MAY DAY

*A Short
History of the
International
Workers' Holiday
1886-1986*

May Day Poster by artist Walter Crane, London, 1894

MAY DAY

*A Short
History of the
International
Workers' Holiday
1886-1986*

by
Philip S.
Foner

INTERNATIONAL PUBLISHERS, New York

Library of Congress Cataloging-in-Publication Data

Foner, Philip Sheldon, 1910–
    May Day: A short history of the international workers'
holiday, 1886–1986.

    Bibliography: p.
    Includes index.
    1. May Day (Labor holiday)—United States—History.
I. Title.
HD7791.F65   1986   394.2′683   85-23823
ISBN 0-7178-0633-2
ISBN 0-7178-0624-3 (pbk.)

Contents

8 HOURS

Illustrated Sydney News.
October 1886

List of Illustrations

Acknowledgments
a   *Daily World*, New York
b   May Day Centennial Archive, Berlin (West)
c   Public Archives of Canada (PA-126377)
d   Fricke, Dieter, *Kleine Geschichte Des Ersten Mai*, Dietz Verlag, Berlin, 1980
e   Davidson, A. B., *South Africa: The Birth of Portest, 1870–1924*, Nauka Publishers, Moscow, 1972

Acknowledgments

The publication of this volume would have been impossible without the kind cooperation of many libraries and historical societies. I wish to thank the staffs of the Institut Für Marxismus-Leninismus, Berlin, German Democratic Republic; Institute for Marxism-Leninism, Moscow, USSR; Academy of Science, Institute of History, Budapest, Hungary; Stadt Bibliothek, Berlin, German Democratic Republic; Library of Congress; University of Pennsylvania Library; Tamiment Institute Library, New York University; State Historical Society of Wisconsin, Madison; University of Wisconsin Library, Madison and Milwaukee; Asociación Mundial de Centros de Estudio Históricos y Sociales del Movimiento Obrero, Mexico City; New York Public Library; Chicago Public Library; British Museum; Labadie Collection, University of Michigan Library; Bancroft Library, University of California, Berkeley; Columbia University Library; Cincinnati Historical Society; Widener and Lamont Libraries, Harvard University; Catholic University of America Library.

I also wish to thank Professor Dr. Dieter Fricke, Jena, German Democratic Republic, and Professor Dr. Herbert Steiner, Vienna, Austria, for the opportunity to discuss with them aspects of the history of May Day in their countries.

I wish to thank Professor David Roediger, Reinhold Schultz and Jules Chazin for assistance in preparation of the volume.

Philip S. Foner
Professor Emeritus
Lincoln University
Pennsylvania
August 1985

MAY DAY

*A Short
History of the
International
Workers' Holiday
1886-1986*

San Francisco May Day demonstration in front of City Hall, 1936

Introduction

The Roots of May Day

"The year 1886," observed the New York Bureau of Labor Statistics in its 1887 report, "has witnessed a more profound and far more extended agitation among the members of organized labor than any previous year in the history of our country.... The year 1886 will be forever remembered as one of the greatest importance in the battle between capital and labor in the United States."[1]

The year 1886 will also be "forever remembered" as the year that May Day was born as a day of workers' celebration and agitation.

In the ancient world and in the Middle Ages, days were sometimes designated for workers, and for crafts. During the French Revolution, a special day in September was set aside as a labor holiday.[2] In the United States for many generations, the Fourth of July was celebrated by labor as *its* day. The practice began in the 1790s, when the first trade unions of shoemakers, printers, carpenters, and other crafts joined officially with the Jeffersonian Democratic-Republican societies in the community, and drank toasts to "The Fourth of July, may it ever prove a momento to the oppressed to rise and assert its rights."[3]

By the 1820s and 1830s the Fourth of July had become fixed as the working-class day of celebrations. It was a day of parades, banquets, and festivals—a day for renewing the Spirit of '76, for drawing up the demands of the working class, for presenting new declarations of independence which would serve to finish "the unfinished work" of the American Revolution.[4] It was a day for toasts: "The Working Men—the legitimate children of '76; their sires left them the legacy of freedom and equality. They are now of age, and are laboring to guarantee the principles of the Revolution."[5]

The older tradition of agitation on July 4 did not disappear by the 1880s, but it was overshadowed by two other dates: Labor Day[6] and May First. On August 6, 1882, the Central Labor Union of New York City resolved "that the 5th of September be proclaimed a general holiday for the workingmen" of the city, and proposed that a parade and other festivals take place.[7] In 1884 the Central Labor Union announced that it "will observe the first Monday of September in each year as Labor Day." It also communicated with central labor bodies in other cities to urge them to celebrate the first Monday in September as "a universal holiday for workingmen."[8] Also in 1884, the Federation of Organized Trades and Labor Unions of the United States and Canada (the predecessor of the American Federation of Labor) unanimously adopted a resolution urging that "the first Monday in September of each year be set aside as laborers' national holiday, and that we recommend its observance by all wage workers, irrespective of sex, calling, or nationality."[9] On September 7, 1885, the first nationwide observance of the first Monday in September as a national holiday took place. By 1899 there were Labor Day celebrations in over 400 cities.[10]

In 1885 and 1886, some municipalities made Labor Day an official holiday. The first state in the Union to make Labor Day official was Oregon in 1887. Later that same year New York set the first Monday in September as Labor Day. Five states had passed such a law at the end of 1887, and soon a majority of the states recognized Labor Day as a legal holiday.[11]

In 1894, Amos J. Cummings, a New York congressman and member of Typographical Union No. 6, introduced a bill in Congress drawn up by the AFL to establish Labor Day, the first Monday in September, as a national legal holiday. On June 28, 1894, President Grover Cleveland signed the measure. The law applied to the District of Columbia and the territories, and to federal workers. This federal act, along with additional state laws, in effect made Labor Day a national holiday.[12]

However, by 1894 many workers in the United States were celebrating May 1st as *the* working-class holiday.

At an earlier time, May Day was a springtime fertility festival of May poles, dances, floral wreaths, and general rejoicing. This celebration of welcome to spring comes down from the distant past. The Romans paid tribute to the goddess Flora with games that began on the 28th of April and lasted several days. Through the intervening centuries, other nations followed the Roman precedent, choosing May First as the time for great frolic.[13]

This practice is still in vogue in some parts of the world, but a century ago May Day emerged as a day of international working-class celebration and demonstration. In the following chapters, we will follow the emergence and development of the international workers' May Day.

View of 1975 Montreal May Day parade organized by Quebec's three trade union centers

IK WERK VOOR CHILI

1 MEI AKTIE

EVERT VERMEER STICHTING
PVDA · AFDELINGEN
CHILI · KOMMITEE
WERELDWINKELS · SJALOOM
WERKTEATER · NIVON

1975 Netherlands May Day poster in support of
Chilean victims of Pinochet

1

The Origin of May Day

In the early spring of 1955, the editor of a periodical published in New England wrote to the editor of the *Daily Worker*, official organ of the Communist Party of the United States:[1]

> I am at present trying to collect details of the history about May Day. I was told somewhere that May Day, as a workers' celebration and demonstration, originated in the United States. However, I can't seem to find out the origin in any encyclopedia. Many Americans look upon May Day as some importation from Russia. We would like in our issue to dispel that notion, if it is a false notion.

The information he received convinced the editor that it was indeed a "false notion," that May Day as a day for labor's celebration and demonstration did originate in the United States,* and that it was "indissolubly bound up with the struggle for the shorter workday."[2]

The Ten-Hour Movement

The first labor demand for the shorter workday was expressed in the movement for the ten-hour day. It began even before the first permanent trade unions were formed in the late 1790s. As early as

---

*Another international day inspired by workers in the United States is International Women's Day (March 8). This event traces its origins to a demonstration on March 8, 1908, in New York City of women workers in the needle trades. At the International Socialist Congress in 1910, Clara Zetkin, German Socialist Party leader, moved that this day of the demonstration of the New York working women (March 8) become an International Women's Day, and that March 8 each year be dedicated to fighting for equal rights for all women in all countries. Under her leadership the first International Women's Day celebration was held in Copenhagen that year. (See "International Women's Day," in Philip S. Foner, editor, *Clara Zetkin: Selected Writings*, New York, 1984.)

1791, the Philadelphia carpenters went on strike for a ten-hour day and additional pay for overtime. We do not know the outcome of their strike.

In 1827 Boston and Philadelphia carpenters "turned out" for the ten-hour day. They believed, in the words of the Philadelphia carpenters, "that all men have a just right, derived from their Creator to have sufficient time in each day for the cultivation of their mind[s] for self-improvement." Other workers in Philadelphia viewed the strike as their own, saying that "thousands yet unborn" would reap its advantages.[3]

These early strikes for the ten-hour day failed, but the struggle continued. In 1835 Boston workers issued a circular urging all to fight for a ten-hour day, declaring: "We have been too long subjected to the odious, cruel, unjust and tyrannical system which compels the operative mechanic to exhaust his physical and mental powers. We have rights and duties to perform as American citizens and members of society, which forbid us to dispose of more than ten hours for a day's work."[4]

It was this Boston circular that stimulated the great Philadelphia general strike of 1835. The strike started when the Irish workers on the Schuylkill River coal wharves "turned out" for increased wages and a ten-hour day. Their strike inspired others to join. Each day new groups of workers joined the coal heavers in the fight for a ten-hour day, and soon every union was on strike. Preceded by a fife and drum corps and by banners reading, "From 6 to 6, ten hours work and two hours for meals," the workers paraded in the streets. On June 22, 1835, barely three weeks after the coal heavers had begun their strike, the general strike was won. The ten-hour day and a corresponding advance of wages for pieceworkers was adopted throughout the city, including the city government.[5]

The victory in Philadelphia was reported widely in the labor press and stimulated strikes for the ten-hour day in other cities. A wave of such strikes swept the country, most of them successful. By the end of 1835, with the exception of Boston, the standard day's work for skilled mechanics was ten hours.[6]

The economic depression that began with the panic of 1837 and continued until 1841 wiped out most of these gains and the vast majority of workers were forced to return to a work day of twelve to fourteen hours. Once the depression was over, the struggle for the ten-hour day revived. It was encouraged by the fact that in 1840, the ten-hour day was established for federal government employees by executive order of President Martin Van Buren.[7]

The movement for the ten-hour day in the 1840s was spearheaded by the New England Workingmen's Association, formed during the fall of 1844. Contrary to what its name implied, a major role in the association's campaign was played by the women workers in the textile factories of New England and Pennsylvania. These women formed the first unions of factory workers in the United States—the Female Labor Reform Associations, the first of which was organized in Lowell, Massachusetts in 1845. They joined with the men in the drive for the ten-hour day. Petitions carrying the signatures of thousands of workers were sent to the legislatures in various states urging the passage of ten-hour laws. Several states yielded to the workers' demands for legislation to reduce the working hours. The first ten-hour law was passed by the legislature of New Hampshire in 1847. A year later Pennsylvania and Maine passed similar laws.[8]

Unfortunately, clauses were inserted into the statutes at the insistence of the employers permitting employers to draw up special contracts with workers calling for more than ten hours' work. Even before the laws were passed, employers were already submitting these contracts to their workers and informing them that they had the alternative of signing and continuing to work or refusing to sign and going jobless. They threatened to send the names of those workers refusing to sign to all the corporations in the district so that it would be impossible for them to gain employment in other factories.

In spite of the terror of the blacklist, the workers fought valiantly to preserve the ten-hour laws by agreeing among themselves not to sign the special contracts. But the power of the corporations was too great. Workers who refused to sign were discharged. When they went elsewhere seeking employment, they found all doors closed to them.[9]

The struggle for the ten-hour day continued. By 1860, ten hours had become the standard working day for most skilled mechanics. In many factories, hours were reduced from thirteen to eleven. In 1830 the average working day in the United States had been twelve and one-half hours. Thirty years later, as a result of the workers' militant campaigns, it had been reduced to eleven hours.[10]

"Eight Hours—More than Enough"

Although labor during the first half of the nineteenth century confined its demand in hours to the ten- or nine-hour day, instances of eight-hour agitation occurred even before the Civil War. In 1829

Philadelphia's William Heighton, a leader of that city's labor movement, envisioned the possibility of an eight-hour day.[11] The *National Laborer* declared on November 19, 1836, that it would not halt its agitation for a shorter working day now that the mechanics of Philadelphia had secured a ten-hour day. "We have no desire to perpetuate the ten-hour system," it said, "for we believe that eight hours daily labor is more than enough for any man to perform."

The first significant organizational steps taken by U.S. labor to secure the eight-hour day occurred in 1863. At its convention that year, the Machinists' and Blacksmiths' Union endorsed the eight-hour day, terming it "the most important change to us as workingmen to which all else is subordinate." At the same time, the Boston Trades Assembly took a similar stand, and both organizations appointed committees with a combined budget of eight hundred dollars whose duties were to start an educational and lobbying campaign for the reform.[12] On October 10, 1863, *Fincher's Trades' Review*, the period's leading labor paper, joined the campaign, and said that "today we have nailed this banner to our masthead, *viz*: 'Eight Hours for a Day's Labor.'"

By 1866 eight-hour organizations thrived across the nation. A vigorous labor press, hundreds of local organizations and the National Labor Union marshalled support for the demand and caused legislatures that had not even considered ten-hour bills a decade before to debate the new system. "Out of the death of slavery," wrote Karl Marx, "a new life at once arose. The first fruit of the Civil War was the eight hours' agitation, that ran with the seven-leagued boots of the locomotive from the Atlantic to the Pacific, from New England to California."[13]

In this setting of labor resurgence emerged a man whom the socialist *Labor Standard* called the "originator and author of the Eight Hour Movement."[14] He was the Boston machinist, loyal member of the Machinists' and Blacksmiths' Union, Ira Steward. It was Steward who developed the main ideas justifying the demand for the eight-hour day.

"Precondition for a New Order"

Steward's main theory was that the "habit, customs, and opinions of the masses" represented the strongest power in the world. Labor's demands were small, he contended, because long hours gave the workers little chance to realize that they needed more. A worker who labored fourteen hours a day had neither the imagination nor the energy to demand higher wages. He was so debased by excessive toil that he could think only of food and sleep. "How can they be so stimulated to demand higher wages," asked Steward, "when they have little or no time or strength to use the advantages which higher wages can buy or procure." If hours were reduced, the leisure time would create new motives and desires. In order to satisfy these new habits, wages would have to move upwards. "Change and improve the daily habits of the laborers," he said, "and they will raise their own pay in spite of any power in the universe; and this can be done by furnishing them with more leisure or time."

Further, argued Steward, the eight-hour day was indispensable for removing *all* hardships imposed upon the working classes and the precondition for a new and better social order. As he saw it, the eight-hour day, by bringing higher wages, would help labor to take the first step "on the long road which ends at last in a more equal distribution of the fruits of toil," for wages would continue to increase "until the capitalist and laborer are one." Hence "the way out of the wage system is through higher wages resultant from shorter hours."[15]

Although an active member of the Machinists' and Blacksmiths' Union, Steward did not believe that the shorter working day could be gained through trade union action. Agreements with employers, he argued, might secure the eight-hour day for small groups of workers, but the great mass of unorganized workers would not be affected. On the other hand, if a national eight-hour law were passed, all capitalists would be required to introduce the shorter working day.[16]

Advocates of shorter hours repeatedly emphasized that state laws were insufficient and that a national statute was needed. Joseph Weydemeyer, German-American Marxist, a Union army officer and St. Louis county auditor, supported the idea of a national eight-hour law:[17]

[Laborers'] interests are identical throughout the country, and cannot be vindicated separately in a separate part of it.... They can expect nothing essential for them from the legislatures of the different States (and) they can expect nothing from that party which advocates the breaking up of the country into small state sovereignties.

Actually, a campaign was waged for both federal and state legislation, spearheaded by the National Labor Union (NLU), the first national labor federation formed after the Civil War. Meeting in Baltimore for its first Congress, the NLU declared on August 16, 1866: "The first and great necessity of the present to free the labor of this country from capitalistic slavery is the passing of a law by which eight hours shall be the normal working day in all states of the American Union."

The International Workingmen's Association (IWA), founded in 1864 and popularly known as the First International, also made the eight-hour day its rallying cry. Two weeks after the decision for the eight-hour day was made by the NLU, the Geneva Congress of the First International went on record for the same demand with the following words: "The legal limitation of the working day is a pre-liminary condition without which all further attempts at improve-ments and emancipation of the working class must prove abortive. . . . The Congress proposes 8 hours as the legal limit of the working day."[18]

Karl Marx, who wrote the resolution and was a leading figure in the General Council of the IWA, called attention to how almost simultaneously the National Labor Union in the United States and the First International in Europe had adopted the same position: "Thus the movement of the working class on both sides of the Atlantic, that had grown instinctively out of the conditions of pro-duction themselves,"[19] endorsed the same movement of the limi-tation of hours of labor and concretized it in the demand for the eight-hour day.

The resolution of the Geneva Congress also contained the follow-ing: "As this limitation represents the general demand of the workers of the North-American United States, the Congress transforms this demand into the general platform of the Workers of the World."[20]

Twenty-five years later, the Second International, successor to the IWA, was once again to transform the demand of the labor movement in the United States for the eight-hour day "into the general platform of the workers of the whole world," thereby creating international May Day.

Laws and Loopholes

The campaign in the United States for state and federal legislation for the eight-hour day brought successes. By 1868, six states and several cities had already passed eight-hour laws. That same year, after a national campaign elicited more than 10,000 petition signatures, Congress passed an eight-hour day for laborers, mechanics, and all other workmen in federal employ.[21]

An eight-hour "Jubilee of Labor" greeted the laws, and Ira Steward inscribed the couplet:[22]

Let all now cheer, who never cheered before,
And those who always cheer, now cheer the more.

But the cheers were soon hushed. The state laws proved to be but empty promises. An eight-hour law had been enacted in New York in 1867, but Governor Fenton refused to help enforce it. When the New York Workingmen's Assembly asked the governor to issue a proclamation calling upon employers to observe the law, he replied, "It would be an act of unwarranted assumption to issue a proclamation requiring its observance."[23]

Most of the laws were full of loopholes. One passed in California provided for an eight-hour day in "all cases within this state, unless otherwise expressly stipulated between the parties concerned." The Illinois law was to be effective only where there was "no special contract to the contrary."[24] After passage of these laws employers informed their workers that only those who signed contracts agreeing to work longer hours could hold their jobs. "For all practical purposes," reported a committee of the National Labor Union, "the eight-hour laws might as well have never been placed on the statute books, and can only be described as frauds on the laboring class."[25]

The passage of the federal eight-hour law in 1868 marked the first time since the order of President Martin Van Buren in 1840 establishing the ten-hour day for government employees that labor's demands had been officially recognized by the federal government. It was also an object lesson in how social legislation governing the work place could be emasculated by courts and federal agencies. Some department heads reduced wages in proportion to the change in hours.[26] Then the Attorney General of the United States ruled that the eight-hour law did not apply to work on government contracts. In 1877 the Supreme Court unanimously supported the Attorney General's position. With the door opened, government agencies soon reinstituted ten-hour contracts. By the 1880s, both the chairman of the House Committee on Education and Labor and labor historian Richard Ely agreed that the federal eight-hour law was a "dead letter."[27]

During the long depression that began in 1873 and lasted until 1879, employers sought to lengthen the working day. Both local unions and the Industrial Congress, a labor federation including delegates from five national unions, vigorously protested the extension of hours as contributing to still greater unemployment. A wave of demonstrations around the issue took place during the depression years. The demonstrators supported the eight-hour system in private industry and demanded that the federal statute on hours be enforced.[28]

These demonstrations were not successful. Working hours remained inhumanly long throughout the early 1880s. The most complete available figures, covering 552 establishments in forty industries and twenty-eight states, date from 1883 and indicate that the average working day was still over ten hours, including Saturdays. By that year a ten-hour six-day week had become the norm in most of the surveyed industries, but glaring exceptions to this schedule persisted. Working days were often twelve to fifteen hours long, and in many industries employees also worked holidays and Sundays the year round. It was not unusual to require laborers to work 24 hours consecutively when changes from day to night shifts were made.[29]

The Knights of Labor: "An Injury to One . . ."

Throughout most of the 1880s, the largest and most important labor union in the United States was the Order of the Knights of Labor, with a membership of over 700,000 in 1886. Operating on the basis of its slogan, "An Injury to One is the Concern of All," the Knights of Labor organized both skilled and unskilled workers, welcomed Black workers into its ranks and included many female organizers and members.[30] On the other hand, the Knights did not limit their membership to wage workers but instead barred only stockbrokers, lawyers, doctors, gamblers, bankers and saloonkeepers from its ranks. In some locals, politicians and small businessmen exercised considerable influence, strengthening the leadership's predisposition against strikes.[31]

The first constitution adopted by the Knights in 1878 featured the following demand in its preamble: "The reduction of the hours of labor to eight per day, so the laborers may have more time for social enjoyment and intellectual improvement and be enabled to reap the advantages conferred by the labor-saving machinery which their brains have created."

From 1881 to 1883, the general assembly considered resolutions to set aside a particular Monday, the first one in either May or September, when "all branches of labor throughout the country shall make a demand upon employers that thereafter eight hours shall constitute a legal day's work." The resolution contemplated legislative action to enforce the demand but was regularly tabled or voted down on the theory that the demonstrations would fizzle and thus hurt the Order. In 1884 the Knights did again declare their desire: "To shorten the hours of labor by a general refusal to work more than eight hours."[32]

But the statements of the Knights were never followed by any effort to win the eight-hour day. Especially under Terence V. Powderly, Grand Master Workman after 1879, the issue became subordinated to land reform and, especially, to the cooperative movement which Powderly promised would automatically solve the hours question upon the abolition of the wage system.[33] While his writings and speeches advanced most of the arguments associated with the movement for a shorter day, they were empty of suggestions as to how the eight-hour system could be brought into being. His main advice was negative. Strikes were to be avoided as a plague that had "done more injury to labor than they can ever make amends for."[34]

The organization thus concentrated on the use of legislative pressure to secure the shorter day. In 1880 a five-man delegation went to Washington to press for national eight-hour legislation, but when it came to supporting the delegation with funds, the Knights faltered. Charles Lichtman, Grand Secretary of the Knights, and a member of the delegation, remained in the capital for six years, paying his own expenses but failing to win over the lawmakers.[35]

On November 15, 1881, delegates representing craft unions, including members of the Knights of Labor and about a half-dozen Marxists, met in Pittsburgh and founded the Federation of Organized Trades and Labor Unions of the United States and Canada.[36] From the outset the Federation displayed a consistent interest in eight hours as a basic demand, but unlike the Knights, it made some attempts to develop a meaningful strategy to implement the demand.

The Federation at first called for a legislative approach to the issue. The 1881 founding convention heard a report that advised, "Grasp our idea, *viz*. less hours and better pay.... How will we accomplish this? As the capitalists and wage-grabbers obtain their end—by law." The report called on the federal government to enforce the 1868 national eight-hour law.[37] As early as 1882, however, the legislative road to shorter hours came under attack by a number of delegates, and in 1884 it came into general disfavor. The secretary's report to the convention of that year included the statement:

"This much has been determined by the National Eight-Hour Law —it is useless to wait for legislation in this matter."[38]

The Marxist Approach: Militant Action

By 1884 the influence of Marxists and ex-socialists in the Federation had helped propel the organization toward favoring militant action to secure shorter hours. Leading delegates like Samuel Gompers and Adolph Strasser of the Cigar Makers; J. P. McDonnell, the Marxist editor of the *Labor Standard* and head of the New Jersey Federation of Trades and Labor Unions; and Peter J. McGuire of the Brotherhood of Carpenters and Joiners had long been associated together in eight-hour struggles, socialist study groups, and various organizations allying trade unionists and socialists. Although Gompers and Strasser had already begun a rightward swing, especially relating to internal matters in the cigarmakers' union, both retained a commitment to eight hours, heavily influenced by Karl Marx and Ira Steward.[39]

McGuire proposed that workers should establish the eight-hour day by direct action. "The way to get it," he declared in 1882, was "by organization.... We want an enactment by the workingmen themselves that on a given day eight hours should constitute a day's work, and they ought to enforce it themselves."[40] At first McGuire failed to win Gompers' support for his proposal, but in 1884, Gompers offered to support (and helped to draft) the historic resolution introduced at the federation convention by George Edmonston, founder and first president of the Brotherhood of Carpenters and Joiners. It read:

> Resolved ... that eight hours shall constitute a legal day's labor from and after May 1, 1886, and that we recommend to labor organizations throughout this district that they so direct their laws as to conform to this resolution by the time named.[41]

The resolution passed 23–2, but did not specify what tactics should be used. When the delegates approved Frank K. Foster's proposal that "a vote be taken in all labor organizations, prior to the next Congress, as to the feasibility of a universal strike for a working day of 8 (or 9) hours, to take effect not later than May 1, 1886," they implied that a massive work stoppage would occur.[42] The delegates were convinced, wrote a correspondent who covered the convention for *John Swinton's Paper*, that "it was useless to wait for legislation.... A united demand for a shorter working day, backed by thorough organization, would prove vastly more effective than the enactment of a thousand laws, depending for enforcement upon the pleasure of aspiring politicians or sycophantic department officials."[43]

"A Second Independence Day"

The idea of pinpointing a specific date for the inauguration of shorter hours did not begin with Edmonston's resolution at the 1884 Labor Federation convention. The idea had already been used in the 1830s by workers in England in their struggle for shorter hours, and was introduced in the United States by John C. Cluer, an English labor organizer, who had come to the U.S. in the 1840s. Cluer proposed a general strike, or, as it was popularly called, a Second Independence Day, to be initiated for the ten-hour day. This general strike would take place on July 4, 1844, on which day all New England workers would "declare their independence of the oppressive manufacturing power." Cluer's proposal was discussed at the New England Workingmen's Association that even appointed a committee to study how to put it into operation, and adopted a resolution urging the local unions and associations "to commence raising a fund" to be used on Second Independence Day. But the movement received little support from ten-hour advocates who concentrated on gaining the ten-hour day by legislative action.[44]

The Industrial Congress adopted a resolution at its final Congress in Indianapolis, April 13, 1875, designating July 4, 1876, as the date for the eight-hour system to go into effect by a "united movement on the part of the working masses of the United States." But the proposal never went beyond the resolution stage.[45]

Just why Edmonston chose May First instead of July Fourth is not entirely clear. But it is likely that he did so because of a practice associated with construction trade unions. In the winter, when jobs were scarce, building trades' workers were accustomed to working for what they could get. Each spring these workers rallied together to compel employers to sign contracts on May 1st, a traditional day for folk festivals, celebrated by a May Day parade. Thereafter employers were expected to pay union wages and observe union conditions on pain of having their work struck. As a carpenter, Edmonston probably decided that May 1, 1886, was the appropriate day for the eight-hour demand.

It may also have been that Edmonston chose May First as a memorial to the great battles in Chicago on May 1, 1867, for the eight-hour day. The Illinois eight-hour law passed in March 1867 was to take legal effect on May 1, but with the provision that it was to be effective only where there was "no special contract to the contrary." Chicago workers defied this edict; on May 1, 44 unions cooperated in a massive parade to demand strict adherence to the eight-hour day. The procession featured floats, bands, and from 6,000 to 10,000 marchers. The following day strikes in carshops, planing mills, lumber yards, packing houses, rolling mills, machine shops, and iron-molding plants paralyzed the city. At the massive McCormick reaper works, employees simply walked out after eight hours of labor. While the strikes failed and the eight-hour law was never enforced, the May 1, 1867, demonstration, which the Chicago *Times* called the "largest procession ever seen on the streets of Chicago," may have influenced the choice of May 1, 1886 for a new demonstration for the eight-hour day.[46]

Hampered by lack of membership, the Federation of Organized Trades and Labor Unions asked the Knights of Labor "to cooperate in the general movement to establish the eight-hour reform." But the leadership of the Knights, especially Powderly, were violently anti-strike and made it clear that they would not support a strike movement for the eight-hour day. Instead, Powderly called for the Knights to write essays on the working day and to release them on Washington's Birthday, 1885, for the education of employers and the general public.[47]

Realizing that cooperation by the larger Knights of Labor would go far toward insuring success of the mass strike, the Federation made repeated overtures for Powderly's support, but they received scant attention. At the General Assembly in September 1885, Powderly recommended that "the proposition to inaugurate a general strike for the establishment on the first of May, 1886, should be discountenanced by this body. The people most interested in the project are not as yet educated in the movement, and a strike under such conditions must prove abortive. The date fixed is not a suitable one; the plan suggested to establish it is not the proper one." The delegates thereupon passed only a vague resolution in favor of the eight-hour system.[48]

Nevertheless, assembly after assembly adopted resolutions requesting the national leadership to fix May 1 "as the day on which to strike for eight hours." A number of letters to Powderly from assemblies endorsing the eight-hour movement added that it should be coupled with a demand for a more thoroughgoing change in the economic system.[49]

Of the seventy-eight unions in the Federation polled in 1885, sixty-nine supported the May 1 plan. This encouraged the delegates to the Federation's 1885 convention to repeat the declaration that an eight-hour day was to go into effect on May 1, 1886. Furthermore, they requested both member unions and organizations not affiliated to the Federation that did not propose to strike for the shorter day should aid those who would "with all the power at their command." The Legislative Committee was entrusted with authority "to put the eight-hour-work-day in practical operation" on May 1, 1886, and was empowered to appeal for financial aid from all trade and labor unions.

This time the officers of the Federation took some steps to make effective preparation for the impending struggle. Machinery was established by which the eight-hour day could be gained through negotiation with employers, and a form agreement was drawn up to be signed at conferences between unions and employers. But if peaceful negotiation proved fruitless, the unions were to resort to the strike. Meanwhile, until May 1, 1886, the unions were to agitate for the eight-hour day through mass meetings, circulars, and other means, and the workers were to be mobilized to take action at the proper moment. One of the many circulars issued in response carried this militant appeal:[50]

> Arouse, ye toilers of America! Lay down your tools on May 1, 1886, cease your labor, close the factories, mills and mines—for one day in the year. One day of revolt—not of rest! A day not ordained by the bragging spokesmen of institutions holding the world of labor in bondage. A day on which labor makes its own laws and has the power to execute them! All without the consent or approval of those who oppress and rule. A day on which in tremendous force the unity of the army of toilers is arrayed against the powers that today hold sway over the destinies of the people of all nations. A day of protest against oppression and tyranny, against ignorance and war of any kind. A day on which to begin to enjoy "eight hours for work, eight hours for rest, eight hours for what we will."

The circular clearly implied that May 1, 1886, would not be like Labor Day, which was beginning to become officially sanctioned by state and city governments.

Again the Federation submitted the program to the Knights of Labor, but the leadership for the most part ignored the appeal. However, increasing numbers of local assemblies passed resolutions calling upon the leadership to support the Federation. "The rank-and-file of the Order," Henry David points out, "was ready for militant methods, but its leaders were far too peace-loving to resort to widespread industrial action."[51]

When despite admonitions from headquarters, the rank-and-file Knights began to prepare for the first of May 1886, Powderly promulgated a "secret circular" on March 13, 1886, remonstrating against the efforts of members to pledge the Order to support the eight-hour movement. Powderly wrote: "No assembly of the Knights of Labor must strike for the eight-hour system on May first under the impression that they are obeying orders from headquarters, for such an order was not, and will not, be given. Neither employer nor employee are educated to the needs and necessities of the short hour plan."[52]

While Powderly was powerless to stop the eight-hour movement, he did succeed in preventing effective and concerted action in labor's ranks. The March circular divided the members of the Order, and although thousands of Knights continued to play a conspicuous role at all meetings held to prepare for May First, they did so in the knowledge that they were going over the heads of their national leaders, a step which many knights were not prepared to take.[53]

The Anarchists Join the Struggle

If the Federation got disappointing support from the Knights, it received enthusiastic backing from the trade union wing of the anarchist movement. In 1880, a group that had seceded from the Socialist Labor Party in New York formed an organization known as the Social Revolutionary Club. Soon Social Revolutionary clubs sprang up in other cities—Boston, Philadelphia, Milwaukee, and Chicago —where there were large foreign populations and immigrants whose new and bitter experience in the class struggle in the United States made them particularly receptive to anarchist ideas.[54]

In 1882 the anarchist Johann Most arrived in the United States. Exiled as a Socialist from Germany in 1878, he moved to London, where he published *Die Freiheit*, and in 1879 abandoned socialism for anarchism. Expelled from England, he came to the United States where he continued to publish *Die Freiheit*, and rapidly became the acknowledged leader of the anarchists. Most helped pave the way for a congress of anarchists in Pittsburgh in October 1883 where the International Working People's Association—the Black International, patterned after the London organization of the same name—was founded. Most, Albert R. Parsons and August Spies, the latter two from Chicago, were the outstanding delegates.

Two tendencies coexisted within the International Working People's Association. The first, led by Most, advocated "propaganda by deed"—individual terror—as the road to the creation of a new society without authority.[55] The second wing, propounding the "Chicago idea" of a mixture of anarchism and syndicalism, developed mainly in Chicago and other Midwestern cities with a long history of police and Pinkerton violence against the labor movement. At the 1883 Pittsburgh IWPA convention, Parsons and Spies, the two leading anarcho-syndicalists, agreed with Most on the futility of political action and the value of force, but they believed firmly in trade union work.

Parsons and Spies joined Most on the platform committee and secured his acquiescence to a platform that accepted trade union work as a legitimate arena for anarchist agitation. The "Pittsburgh Manifesto" emphasized in theory that the trade union was not to contend for immediate demands; but in practice, the followers of the IWPA were often compelled to support immediate demands in order to win a hearing from workers. Consequently the IWPA made headway among trade unions, especially in the Midwest, where the Chicago section, led by colorful, militant personalities like Parsons, Spies, Michael Schwab, Samuel Fielden, and others, penetrated deeply into the trade union movement. Many workers joined the International—Chicago alone had five to six thousand members—and the anarcho-syndicalists in the Windy City published five papers, including the *Alarm*, a fortnightly in English edited by Parsons in an edition of 2,000 to 3,000; *Arbeiter-Zeitung*, a German daily edited by Spies, with an edition of 3,600; the *Verbote*, and a daily in Bohemian.

By staging impressive mass demonstrations and parades and conducting speaking tours, the advocates of the "Chicago Idea" were able to exert much greater influence than their numbers would indicate. They dominated the Central Labor Union of Chicago, which consisted of 22 unions in 1886, among them the seven largest in the city. They participated in most of the labor struggles of the Midwest and helped workers in their battles regardless of their affiliation or social philosophy. They assumed leadership in strike struggles, and especially, in the fight for the eight-hour day.[56]

A Quarter-Million Mobilize

As May 1, 1886 drew near, it became clear that the Federation of Organized Trades and Labor Unions did not have sufficient forces to mount and coordinate a national campaign. Instead of a centralized effort of craft unions, the strike organization went forward under the auspices of various local coalitions. In New York City, the craft unions did most of the work. In Chicago, Knights of Labor leader George Schilling, a socialist, joined the IWPA at the head of organizing efforts. Knights and the craft-oriented Trades Assembly predominated in Cincinnati, while an Eight-Hour League unified the forces of the Knights and other activists in Milwaukee.[57]

"There is eight-hour agitation everywhere," *John Swinton's Paper* reported in mid-April.[58] The Wisconsin Commissioner of Labor and Industrial Relations later recalled:

> The agitation permeated our entire social atmosphere. Skilled and unskilled laborers formed unions or assemblies.... It was the topic of conversation in the shop, on the street, at the family table, at the bar, in the counting room, and the subject of numerous able sermons from the pulpit.[59]

By the second week of April, a quarter million industrial workers were involved in the movement, and so powerful was the upsurge that about 30,000 workers had already been granted a nine-or eight-hour day. As early as March, in fact, the campaign had forced city councils in Chicago and Milwaukee to grant the eight-hour day to municipal laborers. Some unions began with the demand for the nine-hour day and then shifted to the eight-hour day in the course of the struggle. The cigarworkers, who approached the May 1 action as a national effort, successfully demanded a nine-hour shift in January in preparation for an eight-hour movement in May.[60]

Newspapers speculated on the size of the coming strike and some bewailed the influence of "Communism, lurid and rampant" in the eight-hour ranks and predicted that if the movement was successful, it would encourage "loafing and gambling, rioting, debauchery, and drunkenness," and would bring only lower wages, more poverty, and social degradation for American workers.[61] Echoing such anti-labor sentiments, P. M. Arthur, conservative Grand Chief of the Brotherhood of Locomotive Engineers, denounced the eight-hour day because "two hours less work means two hours more loafing about the corners and two hours more for drink."[62]

Meanwhile enthusiastic workers smoked "Eight-Hour Tobacco," wore their "Eight-Hour Shoes"—products already produced in shops working the shorter day—and sang the "Eight-Hour Song":[63]

> We mean to make things over;
>   we're tired of toil for naught
> But bare enough to live on: never
>   an hour for thought.

We want to feel the sunshine; we
    want to smell the flowers;
We're sure that God has willed it,
    and we mean to have eight hours.
We're summoning our forces from
    shipyard, shop, and mill:
Eight hours for work, eight hours
    for rest, eight hours for what we will.

As May 1 approached, the Carpenters' Union of Boston called for a demonstration of all trades at Faneuil Hall to prepare for the great event. The workers responded, and resolved:

That this is the workingman's hour, and affrighted capital begins to understand that labor has rights which it is bound to respect—giving promise that the hour is at hand when the producer of wealth shall claim his own, and freely share in the gains and honors of advanced civilization.[64]

May Day, 1936. Fiftieth Anniversary parade led by banner of United Labor Committee, New York City

Seven of the eight Haymarket martyrs, drawn by Art Young.
Oscar Neebe is inset.

The Haymarket Martyrs

Born in 1848, *Albert Parsons* was a self-taught intellectual and worker who lived in Montgomery, Alabama and enlisted in the Confederate Army when the Civil War began. After the war, Parsons became a champion of Black political rights in Texas. In 1869, he married Lucy, a former slave of Black and Mexican Indian descent. In 1873 Parsons and his wife fled to Chicago to escape the wrath of the Ku Klux Klan. Parsons joined the Socialist movement in Chicago and also became Master Workman of Chicago's District Assembly of the Knights of Labor. Disillusioned with political action as the route to Socialism, Parsons and his wife left the Socialist Labor Party and became active in the anarchist Social Revolutionary club in Chicago.

August Spies was born in Landeck in Germany, came to the United States in 1872, and moved to Chicago a year later. He joined the Knights of Labor and the Socialist Labor Party. He became one of the leading Socialist orators and journalists, but like Parsons became disillusioned with the political route to Socialism and joined the anarchist movement.

Born in Lancashire, England in 1847, *Samuel J. Fielden* was a cotton mill worker. After coming to the United States in 1868, he was an itinerant laborer for three years. He settled in Chicago in 1871, was involved in labor organization among teamsters, and by the early 1880s was a prominent labor agitator. He joined the anarchist International Working People's Association in 1884.

Michael Schwab was born in Kitzingen, Germany in 1853, became a bookbinder and a member of the Social Democratic Workers' Party. He emigrated to the United States in 1879 and became a member of the Socialist Labor Party. He played an active part in the founding of the American branch of the anarchist International Working People's Association in 1883.

Adolph Fisher was born in Bremen, Germany in 1858, became a compositor and emigrated to the United States about 1871. He came to Chicago in 1883 where he was employed by the *Arbeiter-Zeitung*.

George Engel was born in Cassel, Germany in 1836, emigrated to the United States in 1873, and moved to Chicago in 1874. He was a member of the Socialist Labor Party until 1883 when he joined the anarchist International Working People's Association. He was a printer by trade.

Louis Lingg was born in Baden, Germany in 1864, became a carpenter and was active in the German labor movement before emigrating to Chicago in 1885. He was a member of and organizer for the Brotherhood of Carpenters and Joiners, and a member of the anarchist International Working People's Association.

Oscar W. Neebe was born in New York City in 1850, and became involved in the labor movement in Chicago after moving there in 1875. A tinsmith by trade, he operated a yeast business. He was a member of the anarchist International Working People's Association.

See Philip S. Foner, editor, *Autobiographies of the Haymarket Martyrs*, New York, 1975.

THE DAY WILL COME WHEN OUR SILENCE WILL BE MORE
POWERFUL THAN THE VOICES YOU ARE THROTTLING TODAY.

1887

Monument in Waldheim Cemetery near Chicago in honor of
Haymarket martyrs.

2

The First May Day and the Haymarket Affair

When May 1 arrived, a truly massive strike wave accompanied it. It is probable that 400,000 and perhaps a half million workers joined in the eight-hour agitation.[1] Significant strikes and demonstrations occurred not only in most of the large cities, but in smaller cities and rural towns as well—in Montclair, New Jersey; Duluth, Minnesota; Argentine, Kansas; South Gardiner, Maine; Mobile, Alabama; Galveston, Texas; and a score of other localities throughout the nation.[2]

A Day of Class Solidarity

Chicago had the most eventful May First, with perhaps 90,000 demonstrators on the streets: 30,000 to 40,000 on strike, 45,000 already having benefited from decreases in hours, and "every railroad in the city ... crippled, all the freight houses ... closed and barred, and most of the industries ... paralyzed." In what was viewed throughout the world as the first May Day parade, 80,000 workers marched up Michigan Avenue. About 10,000 Bohemians, Poles, and Germans employed in and about the lumber yards held a separate parade, marching through the streets with music and flags. Freight handlers made a tour of the railroad freight depots, bringing out the workers from all but two railroads. The Knights of Labor meatpacking unions closed down the stockyards, and, winning their strike, gained an eight-hour day without a pay reduction.[3]

"Hurrah For Shorter Hours," was the New York *Sun*'s headline over the story on the May Day demonstration in New York City. It was estimated that nearly 10,000 marched in a torchlight procession through Broadway, swinging into Union Square on 17th Street past two stands—one for German-speaking, one for English-speaking workers. The members of each local union marched behind their own banner, with 3,400 members of Bakers' Local No. 1 heading the demonstration. Music, fireworks and electric lights helped draw 20,000 spectators to the meeting.[4]

John Swinton, publisher of the influential labor reform newspaper, *John Swinton's Paper*, foresaw the triumph of the eight-hour movement. He concluded his speech with the prediction that "the workingmen of this country will no longer submit to be dragooned by mercenaries in uniform and by scoundrels in ermine." Samuel Gompers also voiced a prediction in his speech that "May 1st would be forever remembered as a second declaration of independence."[5]

A thunder of "ayes" rang through Union Square as the crowd voted unanimously for a resolution for the eight-hour day, which said in part: "Resolved that . . . the eight-hour day shall be decreed by statute and the economic struggle shall be reinforced by political action."[6]

Eleven thousand Detroiters marched on May 1, and 5,000 struck in Troy, New York. In Milwaukee, 10,000 workers were on strike or were idle because employers had shut down to avoid trouble.[7]

Interracial solidarity reached a high point on this day. In Louisville, Kentucky, more than 6,000 Blacks and whites, most of them members of the Knights of Labor, marched in the eight-hour demonstration. Louisville parks were closed to Black people, but after marching through the streets, the parade entered National Park. Black newspapers in many parts of the country reported the news that "thus have the Knights of Labor broken down the walls of prejudice." In Baltimore, more than 20,000 workers "of all colors and nationalities" participated in the May Day' parade.[8]

Thousands of workers joined the strike wave after May Day, many walking out on May 3. In Boston that day, nearly 7,000 carpenters, painters, and plumbers, who had been preparing almost six months for the eight-hour struggle, staged a strike.[9] In Chicago, Lizzie Swank led several hundred sewing women on a May 3rd strike march. The Chicago *Tribune* called them "Shouting Amazons," and noted that when the march was over, the women signed up to join the Knights of Labor.[10] "It is an eight-hour broom," wrote the Chicago correspondent of *John Swinton's Paper*, "and we are scoring victory after victory."[11]

In Milwaukee, the second day of the strike brought at least 7,000 additional participants. A like pattern developed in St. Louis and Cincinnati.[12] "The third of May will be remembered in Baltimore," wrote a correspondent from that city, "as witnessing the largest and most imposing street parades of organized workingmen every seen in this section.... Twenty thousand is the estimated number.... A monster mass meeting ... in the eight-hour interest was held at Concordia Opera House. About 10,000 organized workingmen were in the line of procession."[13]

Police Actions and Bloody Tragedy

Two events, both involving police action, stemmed the strikes' momentum. The more celebrated event at Haymarket Square in Chicago occurred on May 4th, while the bloody Milwaukee tragedy followed just one day later.

The prelude to Haymarket was a May 3 confrontation at the McCormick Harvester plant. Labor relations at this reaper plant had long been poor, but they worsened in February 1886 when the company violated an agreement not to discipline active members of the Metal Workers' Federation Union, L.A. 582, K. of L., and locked out workers for protesting the violation. The lockout soon brought on a bitter strike that continued into May 1886. The factory happened to be located near the Black Road site at which the Lumber Shovers' Union, 10,000 of whose largely immigrant members had struck for eight hours, chose to hold a rally.[14]

Six thousand lumbermen turned out for the May 3 afternoon rally to which IWPA member and Central Labor Union representative August Spies was scheduled to speak. As Spies' brief address neared its end, the McCormick factory bell sounded the day's end for the strikebreakers manning the plant. Five hundred members of the crowd left the rally to demonstrate against the scabs. As the protesters caused the strikebreakers to retreat toward the factory, police fired into the crowd. One demonstrator died immediately from wounds, and three more died later as a result of the police attack, while many suffered injuries.[15]

This barbarous act by a police force already sufficiently hated for its wanton savagery against labor aroused wide indignation. Spies, who saw the massacre, dashed off a circular at the office of the *Arbeiter-Zeitung*, the paper he edited. Printed in English and German, the circular called for a meeting in Haymarket Square the very next day—May 4—to protest the brutality of the police. The workers were urged to "rise ... and destroy the hideous monster that seeks to destroy you," and to "avenge this horrible murder." Spies later testified that the heading—"Revenge! Workingmen! To Arms!" was added without his knowledge and that his insistence resulted in the removal of the line "Arm yourselves and appear in full force" from a circular issued the following day.[16]

Over 20,000 circulars were printed and distributed announcing the meeting for half past seven in the evening. The protest meeting announcement was greeted by Police Captain John Bonfield with the assurance that the police would "suppress any conflicts."[17]

Workers began assembling in Haymarket Square at 7:30. But with a spring storm looming and several other protest meetings scheduled in various neighborhoods, the demonstration did not, despite the endorsement of many unions, draw more than three thousand. The crowd filled only one end of the huge and oblong Haymarket area.

Spies led off with a short address directed against the press. Parsons, who had just returned from Cincinnati and knew little of the Chicago events, followed with an oration which argued for socialism, urged the workers to arm themselves, but cautioned against individual terror and rash action. A thunderstorm interrupted Samuel Fielden's speech, the last of the evening, and two-thirds of the listeners, including Mayor Harrison, left the meeting. The mayor called in at the Desplaines Street police station, a half-block from Haymarket Square, to report that all was quiet, that the meeting was nearly over and that the policemen stationed at the precinct, ready in case of trouble, should be sent home.

Harrison then returned to the meeting for a short stay. When he left, Captain Bonfield was notified by policemen dressed as workers. Bonfield then ordered the police being held ready at the Desplaines precinct to move out to the meeting and disperse it. At Haymarket, Fielden was winding up his speech to an audience that now numbered about 200 workers. The meeting was within a few minutes of its end when the police appeared. Armed and marching in military fashion, 180 strong, they surrounded what was left of the meeting.

At Bonfield's instructions, Captain Ward issued an order for the meeting to disperse. As Fielden protested that the meeting was peaceful, the police waded toward the speaker's stand. Seconds later a sputtering bomb flew through the air and exploded in front of the police, killing one instantly and wounding over seventy. The remaining police regrouped and emptied their revolvers into the panic-stricken protesters, wounding many, at least one fatally.[18]

In the following days and weeks, six more policemen died from wounds suffered at Haymarket Square. In his recent study, *The Haymarket Tragedy*, Paul Avrich demonstrates that the overwhelming majority of the policemen were fatally wounded in the aftermath of the bombing by their fellow officers—a consequence of the indiscriminate firing upon unarmed workers carried out by the undisciplined police force after the explosion.[19]

The Leaders on Trial: Eight Marked Men

"NOW," headlined the Chicago *Inter-Ocean*, on May 5, "IT IS BLOOD." For years business leaders in Chicago like George Pullman, Cyrus McCormick, Jr., and Marshall Field had wanted to rid the city of some of its most effective labor organizers—the anarcho-syndicalist leaders.[20] The Chicago *Mail* spoke for such men and other business leaders on May 1 when it denounced Albert Parsons and August Spies as "two dangerous ruffians," who were "fomenting disorder." It concluded on an ominous note: "Mark them for today. Keep them in view. Hold them personally responsible for any trouble that occurs. Make an example of them if trouble occurs."[21]

On the morning of May 5, Mayor Harrison declared "Martial Law," and massive police dragnets started immediately. State Attorney General Julius S. Grinnell advised the police that they disregard the law in making their raids; the police arrested hundreds and searched scores of homes, and offices of labor unions, usually without search warrants. "Suspects," notes Harvey Wish, "were beaten and subjected to the 'third degree'; individuals ignorant of the meaning of socialism and anarchism were tortured by the police, sometimes bribed as well, to act as witnesses for the state."[22]

Of the hundreds arrested, thirty-one were indicted. When informers and the improbable victims were weeded out, eight men were selected for trial: Albert R. Parsons, August Spies, Samuel J. Fielden, Michael Schwab, Adolph Fisher, George Engel, Louis Lingg, and Oscar Neebe.

It was largely due to the militant spirit and organizing genius of the eight men brought to trial for the Haymarket tragedy that Chicago was the outstanding labor center in the country, and had made the greatest contribution to the eight-hour movement. It was for their leadership, not for their anarchist ideas, that they were hated by Chicago employers. A majority of them were not even present in Haymarket Square on the evening of May 4; those who did attend the rally had either left before the explosion, or were not in a position to have thrown the bomb. But this did not trouble the grand jury that indicted them for the May 4 murder of Mathias J. Degan and set the trial for June 21.[23]

The mood of hysteria in Chicago infected other major cities across the nation within days; businessmen, politicians, and police officials used the bombing in Haymarket Square to attack anarchists, socialists, and labor organizers.* On the day the news of the bombing reached Cincinnati, the mayor deputized 1,000 special police. Two days later, he called out the state militia. As one Cincinnati official explained: "We do not propose ... to have anything here like they are suffering in Chicago and Milwaukee."[24]

The Militia Strikes in Milwaukee

Reaction to Haymarket in Milwaukee had led to a bloody massacre there on May 5. A large contingent of Polish strikers, mostly unskilled workers, organized in a separate Knights of Labor section, led eight-hour day strike processions that emanated from the St. Stanislaus Church. The processions had succeeded in closing a large brewery, the West Milwaukee railroad shop, a stove works employing 2,500 and the Reliance Works of the Allis farm machine company. On May 4, three companies of militia prevented the closing of the Chicago Rolling Mill in Bay View, but used no violence in the process. The next day was the day after Haymarket, and the city authorities took a harder line. The mayor banned "crowds upon the streets or other public places," and asked employers to request aid if continued production were threatened. Wisconsin's governor reacted to Haymarket by calling out additional troops.[25]

The strikers assured reporters for the Milwaukee *Journal* that they "had no intention of making an attack on the militia or company property, and simply wished to show that they had not been intimidated." As they had done for several days, they went forth to close down the North Chicago Rolling Mill. When they neared the Mill, the militia's commander issued a single and, according to the *Journal*, inaudible order to stop. Then, apparently acting on orders from the governor, the troops fired directly into the crowd.[26]

The final count of the dead stood at eight Polish laborers, and one German worker. In the hysterical post-Haymarket atmosphere, a coroner's jury praised the militia and returned no indictments. Meanwhile, nearly fifty workers received indictments, and some served six to nine month terms for "riot and conspiracy" or "riot and unlawful assembly." The local press fulsomely praised the Governor

*Paul Avrich notes in *The Haymarket Tragedy* (pp. 155–156) that the bombing in Haymarket Square led to the first serious "Red Scare."

for firmness and offered only mild objections when the employers made cash gifts to the militia companies involved.[27]

Gains in the Face of Defeat

In this atmosphere it was impossible to maintain the eight-hour movement, and by mid-May the campaign lost its impetus. A number of strikes, such as the mass walkout of 7,000 Boston building trades' workers, were defeated.[28] Nonetheless, the eight-hour movement was far from a failure. Nationally, nearly 200,000 workers shortened their workday, some by as much as five hours. It is estimated that 185,000 workers who struck for the eight-hour day gained the demand on May 1 and the days following. Moreover, the eight-hour agitation was mainly responsible for reducing the daily working time of no less than 200,000 workers from twelve to ten and nine hours per day. In many trades in which the daily working hours were fourteen or sixteen, a reduction took place to twelve; not a few twelve-hour industries were reduced, and scores of ten-hour trades, especially in the building line, were cut down to nine hours. In many places the Saturday half holiday was adopted; there was an extensive movement for the early closing of stores, and the practice of Sunday labor was eliminated in many, but not all, industries.[29]

It is true that attempts were made almost immediately to rescind the gains, but many unions, larger and better organized as a result of the eight-hour movement, defended their gains. Federal statistics show that the working week of all those who struck over hours in 1886 went down from just under 62 to less than 59 hours per week.[30] No wonder a trade unionist could ask in 1889: "Do you know of any one trade in which the working people are working as many hours today as they did before May 1, 1886?"[31]

The Conspiracy Theory Prevails

The trial of the indicted Haymarket defendants opened on June 21, 1886, with seven of the eight present. The missing one was Albert R. Parsons, who had baffled a police search for six weeks, and, thoroughly disguised, was perfectly safe in a Wisconsin hideout. Just as the preliminary examination of candidates for the jury began, Parsons walked into the courthouse and informed Judge Joseph E. Gary: "I present myself for trial with my comrades, your Honor."[32]

The judge cooperated with the prosecutors to make sure that a biased jury was selected. The usual method of picking the trial jurors by lot was dispensed with. Instead, the judge appointed Henry L. Rice as a special bailiff, and gave him personal power to select the prospective jurors. Rice placed on the juror list only persons of obvious prejudice against the defendants.[33] Judge Gary ignored the fact that one of the jurors was a relative of a police officer who had died as a result of the Haymarket bomb. The result was the impaneling of a twelve-man jury that included no workers but instead was composed of managers, salesmen, contractors, and businessmen—all overwhelmingly antagonistic to socialism and anarchism.[34]

All the defendants were accused of murder, but not of throwing the bomb; they were alleged to be murderers on the grounds that the unknown bomb-thrower was influenced by their speeches. In short, they were charged not with bomb-throwing but with conspiracy.[35] Moreover, Judge Gary forced the eight to be tried together in a "conspiracy trial" on the basis that if one was guilty and the others knew each other and had conspired, all were guilty. He confined counsel for the defense, in cross-examining state's witnesses, to the specific points touched on by the state, but in the cross-examination of the defendants' witnesses, he permitted the state's attorney to go into all manner of subjects foreign to the issues on which the witnesses were examined. He allowed the prosecution to drag in any and all questions associated with anarchism, but denied the defense the right to clarify the defendants' attitude toward the use of force and violence. He permitted the police to display all types of dynamite and bombs, in order to strike terror among the jurymen, and his insulting remarks throughout the trial about the defendants, within the hearing of the jury, revealed his deep hatred of these men.[36]

That the eight men were being condemned for their ideas and not for any deeds was stated bluntly by State's Attorney Grinnell in his summation to the jury:[37]

> Law is on trial. Anarchy is on trial. These men have been selected, picked out by the grand jury and indicted because they are the leaders. They are no more guilty than those thousands who follow them. Gentlemen of the jury; convict these men, make examples of them, hang them and you save our institutions, our society.

"It can and must be shown that all this arming was for resistance, not for attack," Parsons wrote in his notebook during the trial.[38] Gary's rulings made it impossible for the defense, led by liberal corporation lawyer William Perkins Black, to present such a point.

After a short deliberation, on August 20 the jury brought in a verdict of guilty. All but Neebe were sentenced to death by hanging. Although even State's Attorney Grinnell had recommended that charges against Neebe be dropped, Judge Gary gave him fifteen years at hard labor in Joliet Prison.[39]

The conclusion of Henry David in his 1936 study, *The History of the Haymarket Affair*, is still valid word for word fifty years later:[40]

> Parsons, Spies, Fielden, Neebe, Engel, Fisher, Schwab, and Lingg were not guilty of the murder of Officer Degan in the light of the evidence produced in court. A biased jury, a prejudiced judge, perjured evidence, an extraordinary and indefensible theory of conspiracy, and the temper of Chicago led to the conviction. The evidence never proved their guilt. . . . No valid defense can be made for the verdict.

After a motion by defense for a new trial was denied by Judge Gary, the convicted men were called upon to speak before sentence was pronounced. Their speeches, lasting three days, reveal these high-minded and courageous men as true heroes of the working class. Spies spoke first: "Your Honor, in addressing this court I speak as the representative of one class to the representative of the other." He spoke for hours, refuting the charges of murder and conspiracy, charging the state with deliberately plotting to use the Haymarket tragedy as an excuse to assassinate the leaders of the working class, accusing the employers of using the same episode to destroy the eight-hour movement by murdering those whom the workers looked up to as their leaders. But he was confident that this conspiracy would not succeed:[41]

> If you think that by hanging us you can stamp out the labor movement . . . the movement from which the downtrodden millions, the millions who toil in want and misery expect salvation—if this is your opinion, then hang us! Here you will tread upon a spark, but there and there, behind you and in front of you, and everywhere, flames blaze up. It is a subterranean fire. You cannot put it out.

Parsons charged in his speech that the verdict "is the verdict of passion, born in passion, nurtured in passion and is the sum total of the organized passion of the City of Chicago." He indicted the press, quoting from editorials in the Chicago *Tribune*, *Frank Leslie's Illustrated Newspaper*, and the New York *Herald* to prove that these papers, speaking for the employers, advocated open violence against the working class—"the killing of people, when they protested against wrong and oppression." He charged the employers with the bomb-throwing crime, which, he said, had been committed to discredit the eight-hour movement.[42]

The defense appealed, and the Illinois Supreme Court upheld the verdict while acknowledging faults in the trial. The hanging was scheduled for November 11, 1887, for seven of the defendants. The defense then tried to appeal the case to the United States Supreme Court, but that body refused to review it.[43]

All this time defense efforts in behalf of the eight men were mounting. More and more trade unionists now took a public stand for clemency, partly in opposition to capital punishment but mainly because they believed that an injustice had been done. In his autobiography, written in the 1920s, Samuel Gompers summed up the reason for his action in behalf of the Haymarket martyrs: "Labor must do its best to maintain justice for the radicals or find itself denied the rights of freemen."[44]

Although Terence V. Powderly fought any effort by the Knights of Labor to offer support for the men sentenced to be executed, a number of local assemblies joined the defense campaign. The Chicago Knights of Labor, after following Powderly for a time, switched to a position of support for the accused. Its official organ, *Knights of Labor*, made an important contribution to the defense effort by publishing the autobiographies of the condemned men, written by them while they sat in prison. In announcing the series, the *Knights of Labor* called it the "only true history of the men who are CONDEMNED TO SUFFER DEATH for exercising the right of Free Speech."[45]

The newly-organized American Federation of Labor, heir to the Federation of Organized Trades and Labor Unions, passed a resolution at its 1886 convention pleading for clemency.[46] Members of District 49, of the Knights of Labor, defied warnings from the K of L General Executive Board, and, together with representatives from the New York City Central Labor Union, campaigned openly for clemency.[47]

Among the distinguished Americans who joined sections of organized labor in protesting the verdict and petitioning for a commutation of the sentences were William Dean Howells, Robert G. Ingersoll, Governor Benjamin Butler, Daniel De Leon, Lyman Trumbull (who had been a judge of the Illinois Supreme Court for eighteen years); a U.S. Senator, the Honorable Leonard Sweet, the old law associate of Abraham Lincoln; the noted liberal writer Henry Demarest Lloyd; Stephen S. Gregory, later president of the American Bar Association; Murray F. Taley, then chief justice of the Illinois Circuit Court; Lyman Gage, later Secretary of the Treasury; John

Brown, son of the great emancipator; and Moncure D. Conway, the biographer of Thomas Paine. Howells, a distinguished novelist and dean of American letters, summed up the feelings of the entire group when he called the verdict and sentences "the greatest wrong that ever threatened our fame as a nation."[48]

"In the Name of Humanity"

The defense movement transcended national boundaries. At scores of mass meetings English workingmen and women voted in favor of "a protest against the murder of the labor leaders." Meetings of workers were held in France, Holland, Russia, Italy, and Spain, and many contributed out of their scanty wages for the Haymarket defense fund. In Germany, Bismarck was so alarmed by the workers' reaction to Haymarket that he banned all public meetings.[49]

As the execution date drew near, a flood of petitions, many circulated by the Amnesty Association formed by leading trade unions, as well as resolutions, letters, and memorials poured in from unions and individual workers to the office of James Oglesby, Republican governor of Illinois. The petitioners also included a number of Chicago businessmen and civic leaders, many of whom had publicly demanded the death penalty during the trial in 1886, but by November, 1887 had come to support the public appeal for clemency.[50]

"In the name of mercy, in the name of humanity, the undersigned on behalf of the American Federation of Labor composed of more than half a million heads of families, bread winners, earnestly implore you to exercise your sovereign perrogative with which you are clothed by the constitution of the great State of Illinois." So began a letter of November 7, 1887, to Governor Oglesby, by Samuel Gompers as President of the American Federation of Labor. It continued with a plea for the governor to "extend clemency" to the condemned men. "Grant this prayer and you will be blessed by the living and countless thousands yet unborn....," Gompers concluded.[51]

On November 10, the day before the execution was to take place, Governor Oglesby yielded somewhat to the national and worldwide pressure by converting the sentences of Samuel Fielden and Michael Schwab to life imprisonment. It appears that the Governor had essentially delivered his power to pardon the accused into the hands of Marshall Field who blocked any further use of that power beyond the two whose sentences were converted.[52]

Parsons, Engel, Spies and Fisher died on the gallows on November

11, 1887, soon to be known throughout the world as "Black Friday." Lingg committed suicide (or was murdered) in his jail cell.

As his own voice was stilled forever, Parsons demanded: "Let the voice of the people be heard." Fischer and Engel proclaimed "Hurrah for anarchy" with their last breaths, with the former adding, "This is the happiest moment of my life." Spies' last words, now carved on the Haymarket Monument, were: "There will come a time when our silence will be more powerful than the voices you strangle today!"[53]

On the next day, the bodies of the four men were returned to their families and friends. (Lingg's body was turned over to the Engel family because he had no family in the United States.) Thousands filed by the bodies all that day to pay their last respects. Many buildings in Chicago's working class districts were covered with black bunting.[54]

On Sunday, November 13, the funeral began at noon. With nearly half a million people watching, thousands of workers marched with the five bodies along Milwaukee Avenue into the downtown area, to the Grand Central Railroad Station, and then by train to the gravesite in German Waldheim Cemetery in Forest Park, Illinois, ten miles west of Chicago. The sole cemetery in the Chicago area for many years that practiced no racial or political discrimination in regard to who could be buried there, Waldheim was the only one willing to receive the remains of the Haymarket martyrs. The bodies of Spies, Parsons, Engel, Fisher, and Lingg were placed in a single temporary burial place while the mourners listened to William Black, the defense attorney, deliver the eulogy. "We do not stand here by the bodies of felons," he said. "There is nothing disgraceful about their death. They died for liberty, for the sacred right of untrammeled speech and for humanity. We are proud to have been their friends . . . ."[55]

June 25, 1893, following a parade through Chicago's streets and in the presence of 8,000 people at Waldheim Cemetery, the Haymrket Martyr Monument was dedicated, designed by the sculptor Albert Weiner. The monument depicts Justice, represented by a woman, placing a laurel wreath on the head of a fallen worker. Many of those present were foreign visitors attending the Chicago Columbian Exposition. Delegations from trade unions in Belgium, France, and England placed flowers on the monument.[56]

On the day after the dedication, Governor John Peter Altgeld issued his famous pardon message in which he showed "that the defendants were not proven to be guilty of the crime." In pardoning Fielden, Schwab, and Neebe, Altgeld stated bluntly that they were completely innocent and that they and the hanged men had been the victims of packed juries and a biased judge and had not received a fair trial.[57]

"THE CHICAGO MARTYRS VINDICATED," read the headline in *The People*, organ of the Socialist Labor Party, in its issue of July 9, 1893, which published the full text of Altgeld's pardon message. "Workingmen of America." it appealed. "Read this document; engrave every word of it on your minds and your hearts."

Conservatives all over the country raged at the pardon, and the Chicago *Tribune*, the *New York Times* and other newspapers heaped invective on Altgeld's head. But workers and their allies rejoiced. The AFL convention in December 1893 praised the pardon message as "an act of justice." The trade unions, and the Populists—a protest organization of farmers—distributed 50,000 copies of the pardon message.[58]

An excerpt from Altgeld's pardon message was inscribed on the Haymarket Martyr Monument. But an even greater monument to their memory is the fact that the words "Haymarket Martyrs" or "Chicago Martyrs" have become a symbol of May Day the world over.

At the Haymarket monument in the 1930s: Mrs. Ada Wright, mother of Scottsboro victim Roy Wright; Mrs. Lucy Parsons, Mrs. Mary Mooney, mother of Tom Mooney

3

The First International
May Day

After the wave of repression following Haymarket, the American Federation of Labor took two years to regroup before returning to an aggressive policy of one-day strikes to reduce hours. At the AFL convention in St. Louis (December 1888), the national agitation for the eight-hour day was renewed. The convention set May 1, 1890 as the date on which organized labor would enforce the eight-hour day. The resolution instructed the executive council to inaugurate an energetic educational and organizational campaign around the issue. Four days were set aside for eight-hour mass rallies: Washington's Birthday in 1889 and 1890; Independence Day, July 4, 1889; and Labor Day, September 2, 1889. The movement was to be climaxed with a mass strike on May 1, 1890.[1]

The campaign inaugurated by the AFL was militant and aggressive. On Washington's Birthday, 1889, at 240 mass meetings across the country, the workers adopted resolutions endorsing the action of the Federation's St. Louis Convention. On Independence Day, demonstrations took place in 311 cities and towns, and by Labor Day (September 2), the number of simultaneous meetings to agitate the eight-hour question had grown to more than 420. By November 1889, the AFL had distributed more than 50,000 pamphlets and more than half a million circulars, and sent 1,200 personal letters to prominent leaders throughout the country.[2]

Across the Atlantic, meanwhile, labor organizations in England, France, Germany, and other European countries hailed the determination of the U.S. workers and instituted steps to advance the movement. "Although there is no international organization," declared the AFL in a widely-distributed 1889 pamphlet, "there is a manifest international movement in this direction."[3]

In the summer of 1889 France celebrated the centennial of the Great Revolution of 1789 with a magnificent World Exposition in Paris and a succession of brilliant festivals. Connected with the exposition were a great number of international congresses—of manufacturers, merchants, farmers, doctors, teachers—and of Socialists. Actually, because of a split in French Socialist ranks between Marxists and Possibilists, there were two international Socialist congresses convened in Paris in mid-July, 1889. The Possibilists emphasized only striving for what was immediately possible or practical in immediate demands and slighted the Marxist stress on fighting for both immediate demands and an ultimate goal of socialism.[4]

Workers the World Over Want Eight Hours

About 400 delegates, including eight women, were present at the Marxist International Socialist Congress.* The delegates met from July 14 to July 20, and among other things, founded the Second International, the successor to the International Workingmen's Association (the First International) formed in London in 1864 and dissolved in Philadelphia in 1876. The congress also flung a firebrand out into the world, the first international May Day.[5]

Mainly because it was preoccupied with the campaign to gain the eight-hour day on May 1, 1890, the American Federation of Labor decided not to send a delegate to Paris. However, Gompers did address a communication to the International Socialist Congress, and arranged to have it delivered in person by Hugh McGregor, the general secretary of the International Society of Seamen and Firemen. On arriving in Paris, McGregor learned of the existence of two Socialist congresses and read Gompers' letter to both.[6]

Unfortunately the original of Gompers' letter has never been located and, in a rare oversight, the AFL president did not make a duplicate. It appears, however, that Gompers informed the delegates in Paris that the AFL had inaugurated an eight-hour movement, which was to take effect on May 1, 1890, and made some suggestions "in relation to the *universal* eight-hour work day." Both the AFL and Gompers later claimed that the letter also suggested mass meetings or demonstrations in other nations to lend moral support to the

---

*The delegates represented the Socialist parties of Austria, Belgium, Bohemia, Bulgaria, Denmark, Egypt, France, Germany, Greece, Great Britain, Holland, Hungary, Italy, Norway, Poland, Portugal, Russia, Rumania, Sweden, Switzerland, and the United States.

AFL's eight-hour campaign. Gompers also claimed that he proposed that May 1 be celebrated "as an International Labor Day," and that this inspired a historic action by the International Socialist Congress.[7]

He was referring to the resolution introduced by Raymond Lavigne, a French delegate, and adopted by the Marxist Congress on July 20, 1889, the last day of its deliberations. It read:[8]

> A great international demonstration shall be organized for a fixed date in such a manner that the workers in all countries and in all cities shall on a specified day simultaneously address to the public authorities a demand to fix the workday at eight hours and to put into effect the other resolutions of the International Congress of Paris.
>
> In view of the fact that such a demonstration has already been resolved upon by the American Federation of Labor at its convention of December 1888 in St. Louis for May 1, 1890, that day is accepted as the day for the international demonstration.
>
> The workers of the various nations shall organize the demonstration in a manner suited to conditions in their country.

It has been traditionally held that May Day as an international workers' day was American in origin.[9] However, Sidney Fine maintains that Lavigne would have presented his resolution to the Paris Congress whether or not anyone from the United States had suggested it.[10]

Lavigne, at his own request, had been instructed by the Federation of Trade Unions and Workmen's Associations of France to present a resolution to the Paris Congress calling for an eight-hour day. His original resolution contained only the first paragraph of the proposal that was finally accepted—that calling for "a great international demonstration ... on a fixed date." But before he presented his resolution, Lavigne sought the advice of some of the leading figures at the Marxist Congress, among them August Bebel and Wilhelm Liebknecht of Germany. It was Bebel and Liebknecht who suggested the inclusion of the third paragraph that left it to the workers of each country to organize the demonstration in accordance with the conditions that existed in their respective countries. The second paragraph was added later naming May 1, 1890, as the date for the international demonstration and referring to the AFL convention of December 1888, which had already set that date for an eight-hour demonstration in the United States.[11]

Fine concedes that the author of the resolution had no doubt been made aware of the AFL date by Gompers' letter brought by Hugh McGregor. But he argues that "he was obviously under a misapprehension as to the character of the movement in which the AFL was engaged. The AFL had not, at the time the May Day resolution was adopted at the Marxist congress, decided upon any demonstration for May 1, 1890, and at no time . . . did it plan a demonstration for the purpose contemplated in the resolution."[12] But, as we have seen, at its St. Louis convention in December, 1888, the AFL *did* decide that all efforts of organized labor should be concentrated for the inauguration of the eight-hour workday on May 1, 1890. The discussion at the convention indicates clearly that while the specific nature of the methods to be used to gain the eight-hour day was still to be decided upon, a demonstration on May 1, 1890 was to take place. It is true that an "international demonstration" was not envisaged, but that would hardly have been expected.[13]

There is little doubt that everyone associated with the resolution passed by the Paris Congress knew of the May 1st demonstrations and strikes for the eight-hour day in 1886 in the United States, sponsored by the predecessor of the American Federation of Labor, and the events associated with the Haymarket tragedy. The action by the St. Louis convention of the AFL further strengthened the connection between the United States, the Federation, and the demonstrations for the eight-hour day on May 1. It is worth noting that at a gathering in London late in 1890 on the occasion of Frederick Engels' 70th birthday, Wilhelm Liebknecht, August Bebel, Eleanor Marx Aveling (Karl Marx's daughter), Tom Mann, William Thorne, and other Socialist and labor leaders, praised the American Federation of Labor for its work in advancing the international struggle for the eight-hour day.[14] We may conclude that the celebration of May Day as the international workers' holiday was greatly influenced by the American Federation of Labor and the eight-hour movement in the United States—even though the resolution adopted by the Paris Congress was introduced by a French delegate and not one from the United States.

The AFL Leads the Way: May 1, 1890

Surveying the state of the labor movement in 1889, Gompers reached the conclusion that it would be a mistake for the unions to go out on strike on May 1, 1890 "whether prepared for it or not." By February, 1889, he had decided that the best strategy was to have a few unions at a time go on strike. One or two unions capable of waging a successful struggle would lead the way and with the aid of the rest of the labor movement, including, it was hoped, the Knights of

Labor, they would establish the eight-hour day in their respective trades. Every May Day thereafter another union (or several unions) would follow this pattern until the employers generally conceded the eight-hour day.[15]

The AFL Executive Council sent an open letter to the Knights' General Assembly at Atlanta in November 1889, appealing to the Order to join in the common fight for the eight-hour day. But the Knights, under the leadership of Powderly, branded the May 1, 1890, demonstration as an alien and radical undertaking, Even though the AFL had abandoned the idea of a general strike, Powderly charged that the Federation's strategy was a reckless repeat of 1886.[16]

After polling the various member unions, the AFL Executive Council in March 1890 chose the carpenters to carry the eight-hour banner on May 1, 1890, to be followed by the United Mine Workers whenever the union's executive board should decide to take the step. The choice of the Brotherhood of Carpenters and Joiners was a good one; the union had built up a big strike fund for the eight-hour struggle and was fully prepared to battle it out, with the assistance of the rest of the labor movement. The large strike fund of the Carpenters' and Joiners' Union received additional funds from an AFL assessment of other unions. Union after union resolved to aid the carpenters with cash and to march in May 1 demonstrations.[17]

Front pages of newspapers throughout the United States carried headlines on May 2, 1890: "WORKMEN'S HOLIDAY. MANY BIG DEMONSTRATIONS." In Louisville, Kentucky, Gompers rode in a carriage with local labor leaders in what was called "the greatest parade of organized labor ever seen in Louisville. There were about 14,000 men in line representing every craft employed in this city." In his speech to the demonstrators, Gompers claimed credit for the action taken by the Paris Congress in establishing May Day as an international labor day: "I urged them to join with the American Federation of Labor and to unite on one thing, the eight-hour movement, and they did so."[18]

In many cities, the AFL joined the Socialist Labor Party in sponsoring rallies. In Chicago, 30,000 workers marched under the joint sponsorship. One hundred trade unions were represented in the line of march, led by 6,000 striking Carpenters and Joiners. "WE LIVE BY LABOR NOT BY WAR," read one of the signs carried by the Carpenters. "ABOLISH WAGE SLAVERY," was another.[19]

In New York City members of seventy unions turned out, bearing banners with such slogans as "NO MORE BOSSES—WAGE SLAVERY MUST GO AND THE 8 HOUR DAY IS THE NEXT STEP IN THE LABOR

MOVEMENT. THE SOCIALIST COMMONWEALTH IS THE FINAL AIM." The meeting adopted a resolution "uniting our voices with the pro- letarians of all countries" in demanding "that the reduction of the hours of labor to eight is of immediate necessity, and that we pledge our sympathy and support for all efforts of labor to secure that end." The resolution hailed both the AFL and the Paris Congress of the Second International for having inaugurated "a new and final eight- hour movement not to be relaxed until its complete triumph is achieved." It pointed with pride to concurrent rallies in many na- tions, and reminded all who fought for the eight-hour day that they should "not lose sight of the ultimate aim of the proletarian move- ment, the abolition of wage slavery."[20]

The gains of 1890 were staggering. Forty-six thousand carpenters achieved the eight-hour day along with thousands of laborers in allied building trades; another 30,000 carpenters won a nine-hour day. The union enlisted many new members. Between March 14 and July 14, 1890, 142 locals were formed, and added new members during the year, as compared to an increase in membership of 3,078 in 1889. Nor was this union the only one to feel the effect. "Every trade and labor union of the country has vastly increased its mem- bership," Gompers wrote to a French Socialist on May 9, 1890.

Hundreds of thousands of workers secured increases in their wages and reduced their hours of labor in the strikes on and around May 1, 1890. According to *Bradstreets*, more strikes were initiated on May 1, 1890, than on any other single day in the history of the United States up to that time.[21]

Labor's Emancipation Day—Worldwide

The New York *World* on May 2, 1890, devoted its entire first page to coverage of "Labor's Emancipation Day" throughout the world. "PARADE OF JUBILANT WORKINGMEN IN ALL THE TRADE CENTERS OF THE CIVILIZED WORLD," read one of the headlines. "EVERY- WHERE THE WORKMEN JOIN IN DEMANDS FOR A NORMAL DAY," read another.

"Everywhere" was an exaggeration, but May 1, 1890, was widely celebrated. "It is certain," the London *Times* noted on May 2,

"that simultaneous demonstrations of working men did actually take place in industrial centers of most European countries. Dem- onstrations were held in London, Paris, Madrid, Barcelona, Valencia, Seville, Lisbon, Copenhagen, Brussels, Budapest, Berlin, Prague, Turin, Geneva, Lugarno, Warsaw, Vienna, Marseille, Reims, Amsterdam,

Stockholm, Helsinki, and other cities. Outside of Europe there were demonstrations in Cuba, Peru, and Chile." There was no demonstration in the Far East, but in Japan, journalist and government adviser Yuzabaro Sakai published a description of the first May Day demonstration in Paris, which he witnessed. When the articles appeared that July in the magazine *Kokumin No Tomo*, at a time when there were as yet no labor unions in Japan, they did acquaint Japanese labor that a day existed which workers were celebrating in various countries of the world.[22]

Let us consider the first May Day in several of these countries.

Enthusiasm in Germany for stoppage of work on May 1, 1890, grew as many trade unions endorsed the call of the Paris Congress. This increased enormously when on January 25, 1890, Prime Minister Bismarck's anti-Socialist law barring public demonstrations and other activities by Socialists, expired. "What is to Happen on May 1st?" asked a leaflet signed by twelve leading Social Democrats in Berlin. The answer was that there should be a stoppage of work in all industrial towns with strong trade unions. But August Bebel, in a letter to Frederick Engels, opposed the suggestion, arguing that "we have every cause to restrain the masses at the demonstration on May 1st, so that there shall be no conflicts." On April 13 the Social Democratic Parliamentary Party endorsed Bebel's position, not only because of the necessity to avoid conflict, but also because the Paris Congress had not specifically mentioned a stoppage of work as the form the eight-hour demonstration should take, leaving it up to each country to decide for itself the best method to be used.[23]

Engels agreed with Bebel. It was necessary to avoid giving the authorities an excuse for violence against the workers and to institute new repressive measures. Things were "moving altogether too splendidly for us in Germany to have us spoil them by pure braggadocio," and the German people "require a certain curb in order not to make any blunder," he wrote to Friedrich A. Sorge in the United States on April 19 1890.[24]

Employers in Germany began organizing to prevent any strikes on May 1. The Hamburg-Altona Employers' Association was formed in the third week of April, and in a public statement signed by all its members, declared that it had been organized for the purpose of "dismissing and paying off, for breach of contract, on May 2, those workers who, as a result of the social democratic demonstration on May 1st of this year, stay away from work or prematurely stop work."[25] Similar threats were issued by employers' associations in other cities. The Association of Leipzig industrialists warned that any workers who failed to show up for work on May 1 would be immediately dismissed for at least eight weeks and would be rehired only at a lower wage.[26]

On April 13, 1890, the Austrian ambassador reported from Berlin that the Imperial Chancellor had informed him that "severe action would be taken against all employees of the Crown and the State, either through discharge without notice or fines, who stopped work on May 1st. Further, it had been decided to prohibit all processions and demonstration meetings."[27]

Despite the threats from government authorities and employers, May 1, 1890 was celebrated in nearly every industrial area and many other towns in Germany. Observing the advice of the Parliamentary Party to avoid a confrontation with the employers and the authorities, most workers did not stop work in the course of demanding an eight-hour day. But about 100,000 did go out on strike in Berlin, Bremen, Dresden, Frankfurt, Hamburg, Leipzig, Munich, and several other cities and towns. About 20,000 to 30,000 workers in Hamburg went on strike.[28]

The majority of German workers, their wives and children celebrated with open air festivals and excursions. In several cities, the police forbade marches and meetings in the urban areas so the workers had to conduct their festivities in the suburbs.[29]

Workers who had gone on strike felt the reprisals immediately. Twenty thousand were locked out in Hamburg, and all union members received an ultimatum from the employers' association ordering them to sign a pledge to abandon their unions or face a lockout. A number of unions responded by calling their members out on strike, and soon thousands of workers were engaged in a struggle which lasted until the late summer. The workers defeated the effort to force union members to sign the anti-union pledge, but the expenses incurred weakened the unions in Hamburg. However, as a result of the increased understanding of the need for the centralized trade union movement to defend the workers, the General Commission of Trade Unions of Germany was organized in November 1890.[30]

The effort to achieve an eight-hour day in 1890 was unsuccessful, and the continuing employers' offensive against May Day strikes influenced the tendency in Germany to avoid work stoppages on May 1.[31] Nevertheless, Ottilie Baeder wrote of the celebration in Grunau near Berlin:[32]

Everyone of those celebrating with us promised to be more zealous
than ever in freeing mankind from need and suppression and to put
his life at the service of our great holy cause. In the whole empire,
nay the whole world the first world holiday has had the effect of a
redemption and has induced a fighting spirit and resolution.

Vienna—"Ruled by the Proletariat"

The employers, authorities, and commercial press of Austria were
united in opposing the work stoppages on May Day that the Socialists
were planning. They informed workers that quitting work would be
a violation of trade-and-industry regulations, and could result in
both dismissal without notice by the employer and arrest.[33]

An enormous scare swept Vienna on the eve of May Day. The
Neue Freie Presse reported on the first of May: "The military are
being kept in readiness, the houses are being shut, provisions have
been stored up as if in anticipation of a siege, business is at a
standstill, women and children do not dare to appear in the streets,
and a heavy anxiety is weighing upon the whole population."[34] Pre-
dictions that May Day would bring "a day of overwhelming terror
and looting" caused a number of families to decide "to flee from
Vienna with their families before that dreaded day arrived."[35]

On May Day 1890, Vienna was described as "a dead city" with
"silent streets, closed shops." The middle-class citizens "had van-
ished. Instead, the Prater was filled with masses of infantry, cavalry
and artillery. . . . The entire security force was mobilized."[36] Nervous
factory owners were reported to have ordered their boilers fired,
and to have recruited the local fire companies. "Then, in case of
attack on their factories, it would be possible to operate against the
rebels with boiling water."[37]

But the Austrian workers refused to be intimidated. "No power
can prevent our not working on May 1," wrote Socialist Victor Adler,
one of the delegates to the Paris Congress of 1889. "Not the police,
not the military can drag us to work." He closed with the words:
"Our solution remains now as before: We do not let ourselves be
intimidated, nor provoked."[38]

The workers heeded this advice. "Perhaps nowhere," exulted the
Socialist *Arbeiter-Zeitung*, "was the May 1st manifestation more mag-
nificently and uniformly carried through than in our land. Here, and
especially in Vienna, complete work stoppage was practically universal. According to numerous reports which lie before us, even in
the most isolated, insignificant little nests where there was only one

factory, they celebrated. The number of meetings...run to the hundreds, also the fetes and outings....And nowhere a disturbance."[39] Sixty meetings were held in Vienna, followed by a "glorious spectacle," a procession of over 100,000 Viennese workers. "On this day Vienna was ruled by the Proletariat," a participant wrote later.[40]

May Day March—Hungary

In Hungary, then part of the Austrian empire, May Day demonstrations occurred throughout the entire country. *Nepsava*, organ of the Social-Democratic Party, reported demonstrations not only in Budapest, but in Sopron, Pecs, Gyor, Eger, Oroskaza, Pzsony (Bratislavia), Transylvania, and other rural centers. A delegation of farm workers joined urban workers in the Budapest demonstration. Indeed, an important feature of the first international May Day in Hungary was the participation of farm workers. More than 80,000 workers and peasants celebrated May 1st in Hungary.[41]

"At 1 o'clock," wrote the Budapest correspondent of the London *Times*, "the workmen began their march to the park, where each group as it arrived had a place assigned to it by the stewards. Within a short time, 50,000 men were assembled within the open space reserved for the meeting. In front of a large platform a number of flags were flying, with the inscription, 'Eight hours' work, Eight hours' rest, eight hours' sleep.' A hundred female workers appeared in national peasant costume, and on their arrival, they were lustily cheered by the 50,000 men assembled to put forward the claims of the working classes." A Hungarian adaptation of the "Marseillaise" was sung, and a resolution was adopted calling for Parliament to pass a law establishing the eight-hour day.[42]

Meanwhile, strikes broke out in Budapest for reduction of hours and increase in wages. The press reported that the strikes resulted in reducing hours of the work day from 12–13 to 8–10, and that in the majority of cases, the strikers won increases of 20 to 25 percent in wages.[43]

Polish Workers Gain Against Repression

A four-man Polish delegation attended the Paris Congress of 1889, and while enthusiastically supporting the resolution setting May 1, 1890, for an international demonstration for the eight-hour day, cautioned that because of special conditions under which the labor movement had to operate in Poland, May Day agitation might be less effective than in other countries.[44]

The special situation stemmed from the fact that Polish territory was occupied by three powers: Russia, Austria-Hungary, and Prussia. Despite the fact that all political activity was forced underground, the labor movement was best developed in the Russian-dominated part of the Polish kingdom. Organized in 1882, the Polish Social-Revolutionary Party was able to function and slowly grow despite mass arrests and imprisonments.[45]

On March 1, 1890, *Robotnik*, a Polish journal with a Socialist tinge, began publication in Lwow.* The first article in the first issue was devoted to May Day. Every issue carried the following slogan printed in capital letters across the entire first page: "COMRADES! REMEMBER MAY DAY! REMEMBER LABOR'S HOLIDAY!" Issues of *Robotnik* were confiscated, but in the face of repression, the May 1 issue carried a detailed program for the May Day rally and an editorial hailing the fact that "for the first time the working class has named a day for its holiday."[46]

With the exception of the printers, most craftsmen, unskilled workers, and laborers abstained from work in Lwow on May 1, 1890. They rallied in the City Hall, filling the building, while an estimated 3,000 more filled the courtyard, corridors, and windowsills of adjacent houses.[47]

While in almost all demonstrations, the workers emphasized the demand for the eight-hour day, in some instances, other demands were also advanced. In Lwow the demonstrators declared that the demand for the eight-hour day was "premature," and instead called for a ten-hour day with one-and-one-half hour break at noon. They also demanded that child labor be banned for children under fourteen years of age while youngsters under eighteen should work no longer than six hours a day; that night work be abolished for women and youngsters, and piecework be entirely eliminated. Political demands were also advanced calling for universal, direct, and secret franchises, the abolition of the standing army, and gradual disarmament based on international agreements.[48]

Some improvements in workers' conditions followed. Work hours in factories were reduced to ten per day; wages were increased, and trade union committees met with employers to discuss working conditions. In some cases these improvements proved to be tem-

---

*Lwow was earlier named Lemberg in Austria-Hungary, and is now Lvov in the Soviet Ukraine.

porary, for a number of employers withdrew the concessions when they recovered from their alarm. But a Workers' Party was organized soon after May Day, and it observed:[49]

> May Day in 1890 was of great importance because it proved how much the working class developed a feeling of political independence. . . . It was only thanks to May Day that we opened our eyes, and that the hypocritical efforts of our enemies aimed at splitting our new solidarity proved to be useless.

With trade unions and political organizations illegal in Warsaw, the Union of Polish Workers felt it was useless to prepare for any demonstrations on May Day. But with the arrival of Stanislaw Padlewski, one of the three emissaries sent to Poland after the Paris Congress, the situation changed. Secret preparations for May Day celebrations got under way. *Walka Clas* (Class Struggle) was launched to prepare for May Day. Its first issue listed the specific demands for which the workers should strike on May Day: "protective rights for labor; legal protection for working people; freedom for labor unions; freedom of assembly for toilers."[50]

The absence of a demand for the eight-hour day aroused opposition among the more radical elements in Warsaw, and on April 28, a leaflet was distributed, printed in two underground printing houses, which noted that a key demand throughout the world on May Day was the eight-hour day, and that this should be the principal demand of the Polish workers. Solidarity on May Day would help them win an eight-hour day, and through it, new jobs would be created in factories for those who were seeking work. Moreover, with an eight-hour day, the worker would have more leisure time which he would devote to the struggle against capital.[51]

Some eight to ten thousand workers went on strike in Warsaw on May 1, 1890. Stanislaw Padlewski hailed this response as a great victory, and noted that many of the largest factories were forced to shut down. But May Day in Warsaw took a heavy toll. Several strikers were arrested, and a number were sentenced to prison terms of from eight months to three years. Some of those imprisoned were forced into exile after they had served their terms.[52]

The strikes brought no immediate changes in the working hours or wages for the Warsaw workers, but their class consciousness increased, and their determination to organize.[53] In any case, the doubts expressed by the Polish delegates to the Paris Congress in 1889 as to the ability to organize effective demonstrations on Polish soil on May 1, 1890, proved to be wrong. In view of the obstacles that had to be overcome, the first May Day in Poland was a considerable success.

Hyde Park and Support from Australia

In England some workers marched on May First but the vast majority turned out on May 4, a Sunday. Between 350,000 and 500,000 demonstrated in London alone in what the *Times* conceded was the "greatest demonstration of modern times."[54] Of particular importance in organizing the tremendous outpouring of British workers was Marx's daughter, Eleanor Marx Aveling. She was active in the Legal Eight Hours and International Labour League which mobilized the eight-hour movement in England. The League was in close touch with developments in the United States "to strengthen each and every organization having the same aims and objects."[55]

The huge meeting in London's Hyde Park adopted a resolution calling "the establishment of an international working day of eight hours for all workers ... the most immediate step towards the ultimate emancipation of the workers," and urged "upon the Government of all countries the necessity of fixing a working day of eight hours by legislative enactment."[56]

"Why did they demand an eight-hour day?" asked trade union leader John Burns, the key speaker at the meeting. He answered that the workers regarded it "as a palliative of the overwork, misery, and degradation caused by the serious condition of the working people throughout Great Britain, and also as a means of giving work to thousands who were out of work, by reducing the excessive working-hours of those who were working. While thousands were out of work, there were hundreds of thousands of men in London who were prematurely aging themselves against their will by working overtime."[57]

Burns announced in his speech that he had received a telegram from the Melbourne Trade Council saying that "the eight-hour system prevailed to a great extent in Australia, and wishing European workers success in the eight-hour campaign."[58]

In 1856 stonemasons in Sydney and Melbourne, Australia, had won an eight-hour day. Thereafter the movement continued to be successful, and by 1889 probably half of Melbourne's workers were on eight hours.[59] Thus when the Paris Congress issued its call for a May 1, 1890, demonstration in favor of an eight-hour day, the most influential of Australia's unions were already holding large demonstrations to celebrate their achievements.[60] They had their own tradition of processions and demonstrations related to the eight-hour day—in April in Melbourne and October in Sydney[61]—and were not yet ready to abandon them for another day on which to demonstrate.[62]

International May Day did arouse some interest if not actual participation in Melbourne.* On April 30 the Eight Hours Anniversary Committee of the Union Council decided to send a message of congratulations to "labour organizations in Great Britain and on the continent upon the stand they were making in support of the Eight hours movement." The following evening, May 1, a public meeting was held in Melbourne Trades Hall to express solidarity "with those who are struggling for a maximum eight hours law of labour in Europe and America." The meeting appears to have been called by the Social Democratic Club, which from its establishment in 1886, had held annual meetings on May 1 "as a gesture of solidarity with unionists in the United States of America."[63]

May Day Manifesto in Havana

In 1887, Enrique Roig y San Martin, leader of the anarcho-syndicalists in the labor movement of Cuba, founded the daily newspaper *El Productor*, dedicated to the "economic and social interests of the working class." *El Productor* helped develop a socialist ideology among the Cuban workers. It devoted considerable space to the Haymarket tragedy in the United States, and raised funds for the defense of the eight accused men.[64]

El Productor was the official organ of the Circulo de Trabajadores (Workers' Club) founded in Havana in 1885 by Enrique Crecci and Maximo Fernandez, associates of Roig. On April 20, 1890, the Circulo de Trabajadores issued a "May Day Manifesto" calling upon the Cuban workers to support the May 1 international demonstration for an eight-hour day. Workers in Havana were urged to meet peacefully and march to a mass meeting celebrating the first of May where they would be addressed by a group of speakers who would stress the "necessities and aspirations of a united working class."[65]

In spite of threats by the police, workers responded to the call

---

*In other parts of Australia, however, achievements were not so great as those gained in Melbourne and Sydney, and even in these cities the eight-hour day was largely enjoyed by members of the craft unions, who represented a minority of Australian workers. Nevertheless, by world standards, the Australian eight-hour movement had been very successful. (Leon Fox, "Early Australian May Days," *Labour History*, May, 1962, pp. 36–38.)

and marched through the streets of Havana to the meeting. The Havana correspondent of the *New York Times* described the parade:[66]

> The various trade organizations of this city, headed by bands of music, paraded to-day through the principal streets. The route of the procession was thronged with spectators, and the workmen were greeted with much cheering.... The paraders marched to the Skating Rink, where a large and enthusiastic meeting was held. Perfect order was maintained throughout the day.

Fifteen orators delivered speeches at the May Day meeting denouncing the miserable conditions and abuses suffered by the workers. They demanded a legal working day of eight hours, called for equal rights for Blacks and whites, and urged the unity and solidarity of all workers. There were also calls for the destruction of the existing social order and the installation of a "universal fatherland."[67]

Although the May Day celebration was peaceful, the authorities struck back. The directors of the Circulo de Trabajadores were imprisoned for having issued the May Day Manifesto, and tried for violating the Penal Code issued by Royal Decree on May 23, 1879. Defended by Dr. Gonzalez Llorente, they were acquitted. A great demonstration in the principal streets of Havana greeted the released Circulo leaders.[68]

"One Army, One Flag . . ."

Summing up the first international May Day, the Socialist *Arbeiter-Zeitung* of Vienna reported enthusiastically:[69]

> The workers allowed nothing to hinder them from celebrating the 1st of May—not the outbursts of fury from the entire bourgeois press of all countries, nor the decrees of governments, nor the threats of dismissal, nor huge military levels. They celebrated everywhere; such an international celebration as the world has not yet experienced; the whole civilized world was on one great May-field where millions and millions of proletarians assembled in order to draw up together the demands they find essential for the further development of society.

In the preface that Engels wrote on May 1, 1890, to the fourth German edition of the *Communist Manifesto*, he expressed his enthusiasm over reports of hundreds of thousands of workers demonstrating in so many different countries:[70]

> As I write these lines, the proletariat of Europe and America is holding a review of its forces; it is mobilized for the first time as One army,

under One flag, and fighting for One immediate aim: an eight-hour working day, established by legal enactment.... The spectacle we are witnessing will make the capitalists and landowners of all lands realize that today the proletarians of all lands are, in very truth, united. If only Marx were with me to see it with his own eyes!*

*Karl Marx died on March 14, 1883.

May Day demonstration, Hyde Park, London, 1892. Frederick Engels is third male from left. Eleanor Marx Aveling in foreground

4

"Watchword for Millions"
(1891–1914)

Although the celebration of May Day as an international labor holiday was initiated on May 1, 1890, Lavigne's resolution did not in itself provide for the annual observation of May 1 by workers throughout the world. It was originally viewed as "a one-time affair," but it aroused such enthusiasm that May Day was continued. In 1891 the London *Times* already referred to it as having "become a permanent institution."[1] On the eve of May Day in 1891, *The People*, organ of the Socialist Labor Party in the United States, observed that "in two years May 1 has become the watchword for millions of toilers throughout the civilized world. The idea of internationalism, the dream of the fathers of the Labor Movement, that the proletarians in all countries will some day be united, is approaching its triumphant realization."[2]

Samuel Gompers credited "the agitation of the American Federation of Labor" for the fact that May Day was fast becoming a permanent institution for the working class. In an interview in *The People*, a few days before the 1891 May Day celebration, he declared: "May 1st of each year is now looked upon by the organized wage-workers and the observing public as a sort of new Independence Day upon which they will every year strike a blow for emancipation and steadily weaken the shackles of wage slavery."[3]

At its founding convention in 1890 the United Mine Workers of America, affiliated to the American Federation of Labor, declared that the coal miner "has the most righteous claim to an eight-hour day," especially because he was "shut out from the sunlight and pure air" while at work.[4] The AFL chose the miners as the second trade (after the carpenters) to press the issue. But the miners, poorly organized with only one worker in ten unionized, became embroiled in a costly 1891 strike in the Connellsville, Pennsylvania, coke area. The UMW had to default on its commitment to mount a May 1891 campaign to win eight hours. Since the 1891 AFL convention had turned down applications by the International Typographical Union and the Journeymen Bakers and Confectioners National Union to lead the shorter hours movement, there was no official eight-hour campaign under AFL sponsorship on May 1, 1891.[5]

But this did not kill eight-hour enthusiasm. Indeed, building tradesmen extended their gains of the previous year in a concerted 1891 campaign. Other trades in a number of cities quit work to enforce the demand for the eight-hour day.[6] On May 9, Gompers reported that 130,600 AFL members had struck for the eight-hour day on May 1st.[7]

May Day demonstrations in the major cities of the United States were large and enthusiastic. In Chicago, 15,000 workers paraded through the streets to the lake front where over 25,000 listened to speakers demanding an eight-hour day. The resolution, unanimously adopted, declared that the meeting acknowledged "the international character and world-wide unity of the labor movement, and we do first of all extend to our brothers of all countries fraternal greetings and promises of co-operation in all matters pertaining to the advancement of the universal cause—the cause of labor."[8]

In Boston, 8,000 workers marched to Fanueil Hall in response to the following advertisement inserted in the press by the Central Labor Council:[9]

NOTICE

Faneuil Hall will be open all day and evening on May 1, for the use of all workers in Boston and vicinity who are in sympathy with the great movement inaugurated on that day for eight hours as a day's work. Good speakers will be in attendance....

The various organizations are asked to march to the hall in a body.

Among other notices appearing in the press were the following:[10]

The plumbers of Minneapolis, Minn., will not strike on May 1. The eight-hour day has been conceded by the master plumbers, with wages at $3.00 per day.

The Painters' Union of Memphis, Tenn., desires to inform all painters throughout the country that their presence in Memphis is not desired at the present time as they are about to strike for eight-hours on May 1.

Unity in Union Square

In New York City 15,000 marched through the streets in a demonstration jointly sponsored by the Central Labor Federation and the Socialist Labor Party. Several thousand, including 150 small children who worked in sweatshops, represented the United Hebrew Trades; they carried signs with slogans reading: "We want children in school instead of in shops!"; "Down with the sweating system!"; "We bake bread and have it not to eat!"; "We sew clothes and still go naked!"; "We want eight hours, sixteen are too much!" The bricklayers were well represented in the parade, partly because Bricklayers' Union No. 9 notified its members that it would fine any member "50 cents for failing to take part in the parade on May 1."[11]

The parade wound up in Union Square where speakers dwelt upon the international character of the demonstration, and the necessity of unifying labor throughout the world in order not only to reduce the hours of labor, but also to abolish the present wage system. The same themes were emphasized in the resolutions adopted by the meeting. Special pride was taken in the fact that "the working men throughout the civilized world are this day holding demonstrations to carry out the spirit of the call issued by the International Labor Congress held at Paris in July 1889...."[12]

In Europe, Two Celebrations

"Governments Trembling as May 1 Approaches"—a headline described the scene in Europe on the eve of May Day. To the ruling classes of Europe the approach of May Day was a symbol of the approaching social revolution.[13]

The reaction of many Social Democratic leaders was to take steps to make certain that May Day passed off quietly—by changing the day of the celebration to a Sunday which was a holiday anyway. In a proclamation of February 4, 1891, the Social Democratic Party of Germany* recommended to the workers that they celebrate May Day on the first Sunday in May in order "not to give the soldiery an

---

*The Social Democratic Party of Germany was formed at the famous Gotha Congress of 1875 by the followers of Ferdinand Lassalle and Karl Marx who worked out a mutually acceptable program. Even though Marx deplored the concessions to the Lassalleans in his *Critique of the Gotha Programme*, the Social Democratic Party led by August Bebel and Wilhelm Liebknecht was basically Marxist. Later, however, under the leadership of moderate Socialists, its orientation tended to emphasize modification of Marxist principles.

opportunity of bathing their sabres and bayonets in the blood of the workingmen."[14]

When the representatives of the German Social Democracy at the 1891 Brussels Congress attempted to establish their plans for the May Day celebrations on Sunday, May 3, for all parties of the Second International, Frederick Engels criticized this as "stupidity" because of the tendency to formalize the May Day celebrations. At the same time, he acknowledged that the postponement of the celebration in Germany to May 3 was correct. Otherwise a repetition of the Hamburg lock-outs of 1890 might occur, "this time in the whole country and under much more unfavorable conditions." It would result in "the break up of all our trade unions and the result, general discouragement."[15]

Writing to Herman Schlüter on April 29, 1891, August Bebel noted that the authorities in Germany were only waiting for the moment when they would attack the Socialist workers and destroy the movement once and for all. But the workers would not let themselves be provoked by the ruling class and were prepared to celebrate May Day peacefully on May 3.[16]

Thus 1891 saw two separate May Day celebrations in Europe. In most countries the workers stopped work on May 1 with demonstrations for an eight-hour working day, and, in a number of instances, for other social legislation. However, in Germany and England the May Day demonstrations took place on Sunday, May 3.[17]

May First passed quietly in Spain. In Madrid, 4,000 workers met to hear speeches in favor of the eight-hour day. In Amsterdam, a peaceful meeting heard Socialist Ferdinand Domela Neuwenhius speak in favor of the eight-hour day and pay tribute to "the Chicago victims."[18] Austria forbade any demonstration or public procession on the first of May, and directors of all factories and shops under control of the state were instructed to prohibit the workers from making May 1 a holiday.[19] But while some large employers refused to give their workmen a holiday, it was estimated by the press that about 90 percent of the working population of Vienna took part in May Day proceedings. They met and passed resolutions in favor of an eight-hour day and universal suffrage. In the afternoon they retired to the numerous beer gardens in the Prater. One reporter noted: "There were no soldiers kept in readiness in the park as last year, and the police were mustered but in small force."[20]

But in a number of European cities where workers celebrated on the first of May, they were attacked by troops and police. In Italy, a proposal to imitate the tactics of the German Social-Democrats by celebrating on May 3 was voted down by a large majority of the executive committee of the Socialist Labor Party. When the workers of Rome demonstrated on May 1, the cavalry charged the demonstrators. One worker was killed and a number wounded. In Florence four workmen were wounded as soldiers and police tried to disperse a parade.[21]

On the eve of May Day, the General Committee of the Incorporated Trade Unions of Paris issued a proclamation that no workmen should work on the International Labor Day, and that the trade unions and the Socialist Party "will parade through the streets and hold large mass meetings in all parts of the city after the parade had disbanded."[22]

On May 1, the police and soldiers attacked the parade of workmen, the gendarmes charging the procession with drawn sabres. The workers fought back, and only after the military, with fixed bayonets, charged the workmen were they driven off. They soon returned with reinforcements and renewed their attack on the police. At this point a number of infantrymen were sent in but the workers, instead of fleeing in panic, rushed at the soldiers and engaged them in hand-to-hand battle. Finally, after having failed to drive the workers back with their bayonets and butts of their muskets, the soldiers were ordered to fire. Three workers fell dead and others were wounded. This brought the Paris May Day battle to an end.[23]

In Fournier, a bloody clash between miners and the police ended with seven persons killed and twelve wounded, two of whom subsequently died. A reporter described the funeral procession of the "victims of the May Day massacre" as follows:[24]

> The procession was very long, being participated in by a large number of workmen's clubs, with red and black flags draped. The nine coffins were surrounded by the relations of the victims. Many women placed wreaths upon the graves.

Demonstrations for higher wages and better working conditions occurred on May 1, 1891, in Oroskaza, Hungary, and spilled over into other rural areas. Violent and bloody clashes between agrarian workers and the police continued for several weeks. Martial law was declared, and the demonstrations were finally suppressed by the dispatch of soldiers and additional police.[25]

Meetings were held in Germany on May 1 at which speakers talked of the importance of May Day, but the actual demonstrations took place on Sunday, May 3. About 100,000 people marched in Hamburg. In Berlin, attendance at forty evening meetings was so great that the halls were not large enough and meetings continued to be held on the following two days. One hundred and fifty thousand copies of a May Day manifesto published by the Social Democratic Party were sold throughout the country.[26]

"We the Workingmen Demand . . ."

In London's Hyde Park on Sunday,May 3, 1891, the Legal Eight Hours and International Labour League (which had formed a special Demonstration Committee) and the London Trades Council celebrated May Day. Under their joint auspices, a single resolution was put to the audience at twelve separate platforms:[27] "That this meeting recognizes that the establishment of an international eight-hours day for all workers is the most immediate step towards the ultimate emancipation of the workers, and urges upon the Government of all countries the necessity of having a working day of eight hours by legislative enactment."[28]

Engels was present on the Socialist platform, and Eleanor Marx Aveling was on the platform of the gasworkers' union that she had helped in many ways. In her speech, she urged the British workers to intensify their efforts during the coming twelve months "so that on the next May Day they would come to the park not to demand but to celebrate the eight-hour day."[29]

"A remarkable feature of the May Day demonstration at Leeds," the London *Times* noted. "was the presence of so many Jews, who, by the banners they displayed, showed that they belonged to the Jewish Tailors or the Jewish Slipper Makers' Trade Union." The speakers emphasized not only the general eight hours workday but also the abolition of sweatshops and out-contracting, and the necessity of returning labor representatives to Parliament.[30] The resolutions adopted at Newcastle-on-Tyne by one of the two meetings called for enactment of a law establishing "eight hours maximum as the working day." The other meeting demanded an international eight-hour day be fixed by the various governments. A resolution adopted at both meetings demanded that labor should be directly represented in all public bodies.[31]

Under the sponsorship of the United Trades Council and Labour League, May Day was celebrated in Dublin, Ireland, on May 3 at a great demonstration, with 8,000 to 10,000 representatives of fourteen trades marching to Phoenix Park. The resolutions adopted began with the statement:[32]

> That we, the working men of Dublin are of the opinion that the working day should be restricted to eight hours, and we hereby pledge our-

selves to use every possible effort to bring about that reform by legislation and otherwise.

It concluded:

That we, the working men of Dublin, consider the time has arrived when the municipal and Parliamentary franchise should be extended, and call on our Parliamentary representatives to have such an act immediately passed, and also believe that Irish labour should have representation.

The first May Day processions and demonstrations in Australia took place in smaller cities on May 1, 1891. More than 1,300 shearers, laborers and railroad construction workers in Barcaldine and well over 600 at Charleville staged the parades. The eight-hour day was already established and had been celebrated on March 1, but they marched out of a sense of internationalism. "In the Procession," reported the *Labour Bulletin* of Barcaldine, "every civilised country was represented doing duty for the Russian, Swede, French, Dane, etc. . . . showing that Labour's cause is one the world over, foreshadowing the time when the swords will be turned into Ploughshares and Liberty, Peace and Friendship will knit together the nations of the earth."[33]

Another first in 1891 was the celebration of May Day in Brazil, held in Sao Paulo and Rio de Janeiro. In Rio it was a three-day festival of labor, ending with a grand concert in the Teatro San Pedro.[34]

1892—Half A Million in Hyde Park

May Day fell on a Sunday in 1892 so that workers did not find it necessary to negotiate with their employers for a holiday. In the United States, however, most demonstrations and meetings were held on April 30 or May 2 since the committees of arrangement were unable to obtain permission for a parade and meeting on a Sunday.[35] In New York City, 10,000 workingmen and women met in Union Square under the sponsorship (this time only) of the Socialist Labor Party, although speakers from the Central Labor Union did address the gathering. SLP leader Lucien Saniel explained as he opened the meeting: "Owing to circumstances over which the committee of arrangements had no control, our demonstration in this city had to be held on the eve of May Day. Yet, as I speak May Day is born . . . and before this meeting adjourns the teeming millions of the old world . . . will be preparing for the grandest display of international brotherhood that was ever witnessed."[36]

This was certainly true of the great demonstration in London where for the first time May Day was celebrated on May 1. The meeting in Hyde Park was attended by "one of the largest, if not the very largest [assembly] which has ever been collected." The London *Times* judged the size of the crowd as being "beyond all attempts at calculation," but other papers placed it at 500,000.[37] The procession from the Embankment to Hyde Park featured workers from practically every trade union in the city. The description in the *Times* read:[38]

> At the head of the column . . . was a band of 50 instruments and a troop of furriers. The first great division of the procession consisted of the representatives of the shipping trades, headed by the dockers to whom had fallen by lot the honor of leading the parade. With them were the shipscrapers, boatbuilders, sailors, firemen, caulkers, mast and block-makers, barge builders, shipwrights, stevedores, sailmakers, riverside labourers, and riggers. . . . The next section represented the printing and paper trades. Then came the leather trades, bearing many banners, as indeed, did those who have been mentioned before this. . . . Next followed the representatives of the metal trades, then a mixed section entitled general trades, under which category were included tobacco strippers, glass blowers, tarriers, coalporters, gasworkers, bakers, potters, millers, coopers, and many besides. Cabinet and fancy trades followed, and after them came men connected with the clothing trades. Last of all came the men engaged in the building trades, a class including plumbers, potters, stonemasons, plasterers, bricklayers, carpenters, joiners, carvers, decorators and painters. In short, a more thoroughly representative gathering of the trade unions of London could not have been devised. The mounted marshals, who were almost as numerous as the mounted police, were busy placing the procession in the appointed order.

Perhaps the most striking banner was that carried by a delegation of workmen from the Government Arsenal at Woolwich. It pictured an immense gun, from the mouth of which was being shot a huge projectile labelled "Eight Hours," aimed toward the House of Parliament.[39]

Eight platforms had been erected in Hyde Park and all adopted a single resolution prepared for the occasion by the organizing committee. It read: "That this meeting consider that the establishment of an international eight hours day for all workers is the most important step towards the ultimate emancipation of the industrial

population, and urges upon the Government the necessity of intro-
ducing and passing through Parliament a measure to give legal effect
to an eight hours working day...." A special resolution was passed
at the platform of the Women's Trade Union League that declared:
"It is the duty of all women to become members of trade societies
in their respective industries, and ... that all women's unions should
combine forthwith to reduce the hours of labour."[40]

The *Times* conceded that the demonstration was "a great success.... one of the biggest meetings ever seen, even in Hyde Park."[41]

Monster meetings were also held on May 1 in Berlin, Bremen,
Munich, and throughout all of Germany, as well as in Vienna, Rome,
Paris, Madrid, Lisbon, Amsterdam, and many other cities of Europe,
and in Tangier.[42] Unlike in 1891, the police and army did not interfere.
Only at Liege, Belgium, did a serious collision take place. Explosions,
probably caused by *agent provocateurs*, gave a pretext for calling
out the militia. But even there the difficulty blew over quickly. One
observer noted: "The stereotypic forebodings of 'violence' indulged
in by the capitalist press at the approach of each May Day, were in
Europe followed by the stereotypic statements that those appre-
hensions were ill-founded."[43]

By May 1892, a severe depression was being felt throughout Australia. Thousands were unemployed in the main cities, where May
Day was marked for the first time. In Melbourne, a public meeting
of 1,000 passed a resolution expressing the desire "on this great
labour day of May First" to affirm "our solidarity with the workers
of the world." About 3,000 workers in Sydney, organized by the
Australian Socialist League, demonstrated under a League banner
that proclaimed "Work for all, Overwork for none." A resolution in
favor of an annual May Day demonstration was adopted. But as long
as the union councils in Melbourne and Sydney were not prepared
to abandon their traditional labor celebrations in March, May Day
in Australia was observed mainly by Socialists and Anarchists.[44]

Keeping May Day Militant

On May 7, 1893, *The People* (USA) informed its readers that while
many places were still to be heard from, it was evident "that this
year's May Day festivities were more general than last year's; that
the popularity of the day is growing; and that its effectiveness as a
means of propaganda and of drawing the working class of the world
together against the exploiters is unquestionable." Not everyone
agreed.

A number argued that May Day had already lost its novelty and zest. "The May First demonstration here [in London] was very nice," Engels wrote to Friedrich A. Sorge on May 17, 1893, "but it is already becoming somewhat of an everyday or rather an annual matter; the first bloom is gone."[45] The London *Times* predicted that May Day has "lost its significance, and it is more than likely that it will end by falling into desuetude."[46]

At the Brussels Congress in August, 1891, the Second International had declared that the purpose of May First was to demand the eight-hour day but added that it must also serve as a demonstration in behalf of the demands to improve working conditions and to insure peace among the nations. It stressed the importance of the "class character of the May First demonstrations" which would lead to the "deepening of the class struggle." The resolution also demanded that work be stopped on May Day "wherever possible."[47]

When the German Social-Democrats and the British trade unions voted to postpone the May Day demonstration to the Sunday following May 1, a demand arose that a more clearly defined position be adopted on the issue at the next Congress. The 1893 Zurich Congress of the Second International devoted a good deal of time to this question. Delegations charged that the actions in Germany and England were causing the original meaning of May Day to be lost. The Paris Congress of 1889, they insisted, had given May Day a definite militant character. But in a number of countries, particularly in Germany, the May Day celebrations were still being held on the first Sunday in May in order to avoid conflict with the capitalists and the capitalist governments. As a result, in these countries May Day was assuming the character of an ordinary bourgeois holiday.

Victor Adler of Austria criticized the position that the German Social Democratic Party adopted in November 1892, that "no norm, valid for all time" should be set and that the day of the May Day celebrations should be determined by practical considerations at the time. Adler insisted on preserving May First for the May Day celebrations and argued that the Social Democrats in Germany should fight to create the conditions for such celebrations. Otherwise, he insisted, "May Day will lose its significance."

August Bebel took issue with Adler. He recalled that the 1889 Paris Congress had said "workers of the various countries must organize this demonstration according to conditions prevailing in each country." Conditions in Germany had clearly revealed the necessity for the position taken by the Social Democratic Party, and if May Day was to continue in Germany, it would have to do so in whatever way possible.[48]

The Zurich Congress arrived at a compromise between Adler and

Bebel. Adler had proposed that it be obligatory for all workers to stop work on May Day, always on the first of May. But the resolution adopted at Zurich stated: "To the extent that conditions in the various countries will make May Day demonstrations possible, such demonstrations should take the form of a work stoppage by all workers on May 1st." However, the resolution also stated:[49]

> The demonstration on May First for the 8-hour day must serve at the same time as a demonstration of the determined will of the working class to destroy class distinctions through social change and thus enter on the road, the only road leading to peace for all peoples, to international peace.

The Panic of '93 and Coxey's Army

On May 4, 1893, the National Cordage Company in the United States failed. A general break in the stock market followed, and soon the country passed through the severest economic crisis U.S. capitalism had yet experienced, with runs on the banks, thousands of business failures, and severe unemployment.[50] By May Day, 1894, more than three million of a total labor force of five million were unemployed. With two to five times as many people dependent on these workers for their existence, it is clear that a large percentage of the population was unable to procure the necessities of life.[51]

On May 1, 1894, the Armies of the Commonweal, led by Jacob Sechler Coxey, a wealthy manufacturer of Massillon, Ohio, arrived in Washington to lobby for Coxey's plan to put the unemployed to work on public work projects. In defiance of a warning from the police, Coxey paraded his "army" through the capitol grounds. For this offense, he and Carl Browne, another leader of the Commonwealers, were arrested and punished by a twenty-day imprisonment and, in addition, were fined $5 each for walking on the grass.[52]

The demonstration of Coxey's Army on May 1 was not linked to May Day, but at demonstrations that day throughout the United States, the police brutality and arrest of the leaders of the unemployed in Washington were denounced in speeches and resolutions. At the May Day demonstration in New York City, Daniel De Leon, leader of the Socialist Labor Party, told an audience of 10,000 in Union Square:[53]

> Coxey's Army had this day been hustled off the steps of the national capitol; but another more gigantic, more powerful army is forming throughout the land whose representatives will soon march up those

steps and not be hustled off; they will be the representatives of the nation armed with a Socialist mandate to wipe out the infamy of capitalist domination.

Speakers, including leaders of several trade unions and of the Socialist Labor Party, pointed out that widespread unemployment made the adoption of the eight-hour day "an imperative necessity." "We demand the eight-hour day," declared Fred Schaefer of the Cigar Makers' International Union, "not only to increase employment but as a step in the direction of the abolition of the wage system through which unemployment will forever be ended."[54]

The resolutions adopted by the meeting sent fraternal greetings to the workers assembled throughout the world "on this 1st of May to assert the solidarity of labor, and urges upon them to neglect no means toward their emancipation from wage-slavery and work unceasingly for the establishment of the Co-operative Commonwealth in which all the instruments of industry will be owned and controlled by the Commonwealth, industrially organized." The resolution, declared the chairman of the meeting, had "been suggested by our staunch comrades, the English Social Democratic Federation."[55]

This Social Democratic Federation* had decided that the first Sunday in May did not come within the meaning of the resolution passed at the International Congress in Zurich, and held its May Day celebration in Hyde Park on May 1, 1894. Slogans carried by the demonstrators included: "Work for All, Overwork for None," "Justice, Not Charity," "English Workmen's Children Send Fraternal Greetings to Children of the World." What was described as the most interesting of the leaflets distributed at the meeting was a design by Walter Crane, "The Workers' Maypole—an offering for May Day, 1894."** It depicted a woman's figure suspended at the top holding a scroll

---

*The Social Democratic Federation was a Marxist organization founded in 1881 in England by Henry M. Hyndman.

**Walter Crane (1845–1915), British illustrator, primarily known for his illustrations of children's books, was an active Socialist, and contributed weekly cartoons for the socialist periodicals *Justice* and *The Commonweal*. For the 1895 May Day demonstration in London, Walter Crane prepared a leaflet which was entitled "A Garland For May Day, 1895. Dedicated to the Workers by Walter Crane." It showed a woman representing Liberty holding a huge garland on which were bound papers bearing such symbols as: "The Cause of Labour is the Hope of the World"; "Solidarity of Labour"; "Production for Use Not For Profit"; "No Child Toilers"; "England Should Feed Her Own People"; "Shorten Working Day & Lengthen Life"; "Cooperation & Emulation Not Competition"; "Hope in Work & Joy in Leisure"; "Art & Enjoyment for All"; "Socialism Means The Most Helpful Happy Life For All." (London *Times*, May 2, 1895.)

with the words "Socialization, Solidarity, Humanity"—and from her raiment streamed ribands [ribbons] with various slogans inscribed on them: "No Starving Children in the Board Schools"; "Leisure for All"; "The Land for the People"; "Abolition of Privilege."[56]

May Day 1894 passed quietly in Europe. In Germany there was no attempt to make May First a general workman's holiday and no strikes took place. *Vorwarts*, central organ of German Social Democracy, issued a special edition that included a poem in honor of the May Day festival and an article condemning the Anarchists for attempting to incite the police and army to disperse workers' gatherings on the first of May.[57]

A report from Austria noted that it was "generally agreed that the demonstration this May First was the largest that has taken place in Vienna since May Day began to be celebrated as a labour festival." Resolutions were adopted at all meetings calling for "the fixing of eight hours as the *maximum* day's labour in all trades," together with "the 36 hours' Sunday rest; the guarantee of the right to organize, and the abolition of the existing restrictions of the right of public meeting and association, together with the punishment of any officials for any illegal hindrances in the struggle over wages; and the abolition of all restrictions on the free expression of opinion in writing or speech."[58]

In Lisbon there was "an almost entire cessation of work," and at many meetings, workers adopted eight-hour-day resolutions. In Madrid, however, the workers were reported to be "nearly all doing a full day's work," and only one meeting, that of the Socialists, were held.[59] In Paris the cessation of work was described as "very partial," and a reporter wrote from the city: "The once dreaded May Day has in Paris, been scarcely distinguishable from any other day. The reports from the provinces also show a marked falling off in the celebration."[60] After studying the reports from its various correspondents, the London *Times* editorialized on May 2, 1894:

> May Day has passed without any demonstration of alarming character. Indeed the accounts from the different European capitals are positively tame. . . . The most notable exception is perhaps the scuffle at Washington where the Coxeyites were rather severely handled by the police. These Coxeyites are among the mildest of May-day demonstrators, but they had to deal with what is probably the most truculent police in the civilized world.

The fixing of May 1st in 1894 for the May Day demonstration in England (not the first Sunday in May) by the Social Democratic

Federation, was followed in 1895 by the adoption of a resolution at the meeting in Hyde Park, stating: "That the workers demonstrating and making holiday upon the 1st of May pledge themselves to do their utmost every year to make Labour Day more and more a complete holiday, not granted by the antagonist master-class, but wrung from them, send fraternal greetings to their fellow-soldiers, the workers of all countries; declare that the legal eight hours day and universal suffrage as two of the most immediate steps to be taken towards the ultimate goal of the working class movement, and again record the fact that this ultimate goal is the ending of the class war by the abolition of classes, the ending of the capitalistic system by the abolition of private property in the means of production and distribution." The resolution was adopted during a heavy downpour, which reduced the size of the meeting, and after speeches by Tom Mann, Eleanor Marx Aveling, William Morris and others.[61]

The German Social Democratic Party followed suit in establishing May Day as a militant workers' holiday. With the waning of the economic crisis, the demand for a stoppage of work on May 1st again came to the fore. On May 1, 1895, Bebel wrote to an Austrian Social Democrat:[62]

> The idea of the May Day celebrations has taken root ineradicably in Germany.... The stoppage of work on the day of celebration is, slowly but surely, being more and more adopted. The sad economic state of affairs which we have been experiencing for years and which hardly admits improvement forces hundreds of thousands to rest not only on Mayday, but also before and after. This is the main reason why the party has up to now declined to take a strong stand on the extension of the stoppage of work on May 1st. But the idea is extending further and further, the number of participants is becoming larger and larger and thus the Mayday Celebrations are becoming, to an ever increasing degree, a proletarian holiday which is dedicated to the demands of the proletariat for working hours, working and living conditions worthy of human beings.

The Party Conference held at Gotha in October 1896 reflected this feeling. In accordance with the 1889 resolution at the Paris Congress, it declared that the "party considers a general stoppage of work as the worthiest way to celebrate May 1st. The party, therefore, makes it the duty of the workers and workers' organizations to support a general stoppage of work, together with other proclamations, and everywhere where it is possible to stop work to do so."[63]

Awakening in Russia

The first May Day celebration in Russia took place on May 5, 1891 when the workers of St. Petersburg held a demonstration. In the years 1892–1894, May Day was celebrated on the first of May in St. Petersburg and a few other cities. In 1895, the Moscow workers joined the celebrations on May 1st under the leadership of the Union of Workers, a Marxist organization established during the previous year. That year the first of May was also celebrated in Warsaw, Gomil, Minsk, and Novgorod.[64]

While in prison in 1896, V. I. Lenin wrote a May Day leaflet for the St. Petersburg League of Struggle for the Emancipation of the Working Class. Two thousand copies were distributed among workers in forty factories of St. Petersburg. "Our bosses push down wages," Lenin wrote, "force us to work overtime, place unjust fines upon us—in a word oppress us in every way. And then when we give voice to our dissatisfaction we are thrown into prison without further ado." After noting the activities of the League of Struggle for the Emancipation of the Working Class, Lenin called upon the Russian workers to join "our fellow workers of other lands in the struggle—under a common flag bearing the words: 'Workers of all countries unite!' " He then pointed to the significance of May Day:[65]

In France, England, Germany and other lands where the workers have already closed their ranks and won important rights, the First of May is a general holiday of all labor.

The workers leave the dark factories and parade the main streets in well-ordered lines with flags and music. They show their masters their power grown strong and join in numerous crowded assemblies to listen to speeches in which the victories achieved over the bosses are recounted and the plans for future struggles are developed....

Comrades, if we fight unitedly and together, then the time is not far off when we too will be in a position openly to join the common struggle of the workers of all lands, without distinction of race or creed, against the capitalists of the whole world.

A month and a half later, when the great textile strike of 40,000 workers broke out in St. Petersburg, the strikers told the organizers that the first impetus was given by the modest little May Day leaflet.[66] As the *New York Times* pointed out years later: "May Day strikes and demonstrations in Russia before the revolution became a political school for millions of toilers."[67]

Wearing Red—A May Day Tradition

By the turn of the nineteenth century, a fixed format had been established for the May Day celebration in most European countries. This format was often modelled on that used in Germany, which had the strongest Social Democratic Party in Europe. On the eve of the first of May, German Socialist newspapers, usually of eight pages, appeared in editions of several hundred thousand. On the front page and the folding inner pages were large drawings with allegorical representations of the First of May, proletarian internationalism, the eight-hour day and other demands, and the inclusion of women workers and farm laborers in the class struggle. Some drawings were by noted artists such as Walter Crane and Max Slevag.

The May Day newspaper usually contained written contributions such as an editorial, a poem, a gossip column, and a short story— all concerned with the First of May. Articles aimed directly at women workers, miners, and agricultural workers usually appeared. Demonstrators bought a ticket (usually for ten to twenty pfennigs) that paid for the Mayday newspaper and served as a demonstration badge.

Demonstrators also wore a red handkerchief, a small red band, a red flower in the buttonhole, a red feather, or a ticket with a large eight on a hat. Wearing a red tie was also a favorite.

Thousands of workers, especially in Berlin, took part in trade union meetings on May Day morning. Then, where it was not forbidden by the authorities, the workers held large processions. If processions were prohibited, the workers organized mass walks during which individual groups merged and the procession of "walkers" grew larger and larger.

In the afternoon the May Day program began, organized by the Social Democratic Party, which became a true folk festival. Members of the workers' Singing Union sang work and freedom songs. After an official address, a theatrical production often followed, as well as gymnastic displays, poetry readings, amusement for the children, dancing, and fireworks.[68]

In London, the May Day celebration began with a procession to Hyde Park. From the Embankment in the afternoon, with banners flying and bands playing, the demonstrators marched across the Strand, through Kingsway, Holborn, and Oxford Street, past the Marble Arch to the park. Here at a number of platforms, each representing a particular union or group, or the Socialist Democratic Federation, speakers addressed the audience. Usually at half past five, a bugle was sounded and a common resolution was presented and adopted at each platform.[69]

Workers Broaden Their Demands

Although May Day as an international workers' holiday originated in the demand for the eight-hour day, by 1891 it had broadened to include other demands, such as: universal suffrage; against imperialist war and colonial oppression; the right to organize; freeing of political prisoners; and the right to political and economic organization of the working class. "The May Day demonstrations," observed a Socialist paper in 1893, "are intended to voice the immediate and future aspirations of the proletariat, together with its international solidarity."[70]

However, the eight-hour day continued to play a special role in winning over workers who were not Socialists. Indeed, Lenin criticized the leaders of the Russian Revolutionary movement in Kharkov for joining the demand for the 8-hour day "with other minor and purely economic demands." In the preface to a pamphlet, *May Days in Kharkov*, published in November 1900, Lenin wrote:[71]

The first of these demands [8-hour day] is the general demand put forward by the proletariat in all countries. The fact that this demand was put forward indicates that the advanced workers of Kharkov realize their solidarity with the international socialist labor movement. But precisely for this reason a demand like this should not have been included among minor demands like better treatment by foremen, or a ten percent increase in wages. The demand for an eight-hour day, however, is the demand of the whole proletariat, presented, not to individual employers, but to the government as the representative of the whole of the present-day social and political system, to the capitalist class as a whole, the owners of all the means of production.

Nevertheless, there was often an idealization of the eight-hour day; it was extolled as the remedy for unemployment, for the increase of wages, and even as the road to the final emancipation of the working class. A German Social Democratic broad-sheet of 1897–1898 and distributed on the first of May stated that "the misery of the workers all over the world stemmed from the same cause" rooted in their daily working hours being too long.

This view was challenged. In a German Social-Democratic pamphlet on eight hours published in 1901, Adolf Braun replied to the question: "What can the eight-hour day not do?"[72]

The capitalist way of production remains in being. . . . The worker remains a proletarian without possessions and the means of production remain the monopoly of a relatively small number of capitalists, just as the advantages of increased productivity by the workers will chiefly play into the hands of the employers. Exploitation and oppression of the wage earner will remain.

Although the view that the eight-hour day by itself would bring on the new social order continued to be criticized, the more common view in May Day resolutions was that it was a step toward emancipation.

"Without Injury to the Workers!"

At the Amsterdam Congress in 1904, the Second International spoke for the last time on the question of May Day. After reviewing the various political slogans that were employed in some countries and calling attention to the fact that in some countries these demonstrations were still taking place on Sunday instead of May First, the resolution concluded:[73]

The International Socialist Congress in Amsterdam calls upon all Social-Democratic Party organizations and trade unions of all countries to demonstrate energetically on May First for the legal establishment of the 8-hour day, for the class demands of the proletariat, and for universal peace. The most effective way of demonstrating on May First is by stoppage of work. The Congress therefore makes it mandatory upon the proletarian organizations of all countries to stop work on May First, wherever it is possible without injury to the workers.

"Without injury to the workers!" In several countries this goal became increasingly difficult to achieve, as the reactionary ruling circles were determined to prevent strikes and demonstrations when each May Day came around. On May Day, 1905, Russian workers in St. Petersburg gathered around the Royal Palace in hope of having their representatives talk with the Czar and protest against the starvation resulting from the Russo-Japanese war then in progress. Instead of talking with the people, the Czar sent troops to deal with them. The troops swept down on the men, women, and children in the crowd, killing hundreds. "This," wrote one historian, "would make May Day not just a memorial for the 'Martyrs of Chicago' but one for the murdered workers of St. Petersburg as well."[74]

Indeed, to the workers of Warsaw as well. In 1905, the Cossack cavalry attacked the orderly May Day demonstrators, and when they withdrew, the infantry fired a volley into the crowd. "Nearly thirty persons were killed on the spot," wrote the Warsaw reporter for the London *Times*.[75] The *New York Times* noted: "Nearly one hundred persons were killed or wounded by the troops. Many women and children are among the dead and dying. Many of those who were killed or wounded were shot in the back; they were running away when they were struck."[76]

Blood also flowed in Buenos Aires, Argentina, on May 1, 1909. Police fired on May Day demonstrators, killing five outright and seriously wounding twelve, of whom seven more died. The Socialist Party and the labor federations voted immediately to call a general strike for May 3 to protest the May Day massacre. Placing all responsibility for the killings on the shoulders of the police, they demanded the dismissal of the chief of police and an inquiry for the punishment of the guilty persons.[77]

Two hundred thousand workers responded to the strike call, and the press described the walkout as "practically general." The strike was supported in Tucuman, Rosario, La Plata, Gardoba and other cities. On the first day of the strike in Buenos Aires, the Workmen's Federation and the Union of Workers demonstrated in front of the morgue where the bodies of the May Day victims were being held. Thousands of trade unionists and Socialists followed the coffins to the cemetery.[78]

"Paris today has resembled an armed camp," wrote the correspondent of the London *Times* on May Day, 1910. "The ordinary garrison of the capital had been reinforced by six regiments of cavalry and four regiments of infantry which had been drafted from neighboring provincial towns. The number of men under arms was nearly 20,000. A large proportion of this infantry force was stationed in the Bois de Bologne and along the avenues which lead to and from the Place de l'Etoile."[79] The huge number of armed forces had been mobilized to prevent workers in Paris from organizing a procession on May Day.

On the eve of May 1 the trade union leaders of Paris had asked to meet with Prime Minister Aristide Briand to obtain permission for a May Day procession after the open-air meeting. They declared that they would be willing to be escorted by the police. Briand refused to receive the delegation, justifying his action by charging that the union leaders had "organized their demonstration and had announced it with menace and provocation, thereby investing it from the outset with the character of disorder." When the delegation reported this response to the General Confederation of Labor, the managing board announced that they would go ahead with the meeting, but because of this "criminal reply" from the Prime Minister, would abandon plans for a procession so as to avoid a massacre. The workers were advised merely to saunter on the boulevards. The statement concluded:[80]

> The union of the Seine Trade Union organizations draws a lesson from the incident. The union will not forget. The labouring classes have been outraged and insulted. They will take their revenge. The principles of liberty demand it.

A number of workers did try to organize a procession, but they were promptly dispersed by the armed forces; most were arrested. Headlines in the press on May 2 read: "Mailed Hand Gives Paris Quiet Day. In Face of Premier's Firmness and Show of Troops, Revolutionists Give Up Parade."[81]

On May 1, 1911, the Seine labor organizations issued a general order to their members bidding them to defy the authorities and vindicate their right to indulge in a "peaceable" demonstration on the streets of Paris. May Day would be celebrated at meetings in the morning and afternoon. But troops occupied the areas that the labor unions had chosen for these events, and workers were "arrested in droves."[82]

On May Day, 1912, about 170,000 Russian workers stopped work and came out into the streets to challenge tsarist reaction. "The great May strike of workers all over Russia," wrote Lenin, "and the street demonstrations connected with it, the revolutionary proclamations, the revolutionary speeches to the working masses, show clearly that Russia has once more entered the period of a rising revolutionary situation."[83]

The First of May 1914 saw 280,000 people demonstrating in the May Day strike in St. Petersburg, 86,000 in Transcaucasia, 44,000 in Riga, over 40,000 in Moscow, 16,000 in Reval, 15,000 in Kharkov, and 9,200 in Nizhni-Novgorod and Sormova—a total of over 500,000 throughout Russia.[84]

May Day and Labor Day

From the first May Day in 1886, the U.S. press has compared the character of the demonstrations on May Day and on Labor Day. May Day participants were described as representing the "European type," while the Labor Day parade was "a demonstration of the honest American workingman." May Day marchers were "wild-eyed agitators," while those who marched on Labor Day were "sober, clean, quiet," and "well-clothed and well-appearing men." May Day participants were "radicals, mostly socialists and anarchists," while Labor Day paraders were "secure and conservative in their association."[85] A description of a May Day meeting in the *New York Times* usually included the following or a variation of it: "Some few among the several thousand, unlike a meeting on Labor Day, seemed to be American-born, but accents and foreign mannerisms predominated."[86]

When Labor Day became a national holiday in 1894, the commercial press in the United States pointed out that while European labor had a class holiday on May 1st, the nation as a whole paid its respect to the role of labor in the United States. The papers urged the American Federation of Labor to continue observing the first Monday in September, but to have nothing to do with the European practice of celebrating May First as a labor holiday.[87]

At first Gompers resisted this pressure. He was still proud, as he put it, that the AFL had supplied the Paris Congress of 1889 with the date for the international labor holiday. On the eve of May Day, 1897, the *American Federationist* carried the following notice: "May 1, 1898—Prepare for it. That date has been set for the general enforcement of the eight-hour work day among all labor in the United States."[88]

Modelled on the 1890 plan, the campaign for May 1, 1898, included a series of meetings on national holidays and the issuance of pamphlets to be climaxed with eight-hour strikes on the target date, led by one union to be chosen by the AFL and supported by other affiliates. But the Executive Council did not pick a union willing to strike, and May 1, 1898 passed uneventfully.[89] By 1901 the AFL abandoned any mention of May Day strikes, and recommended only "discussion and commendation" of eight-hour efforts.[90]

The retreat of the AFL leadership from large-scale, nationally coordinated eight-hour campaigns stemmed from the triumph in the early 1890s of craft unionism and class collaboration. Moreover, the struggle against Socialists inside the AFL made the radical and international aspects of May Day seem a liability to conservative unionists. Soon the leadership of the AFL disowned May Day as a workers' holiday, claiming that it belonged to Europe and the socialists rather than to the United States and U.S. trade unions. They ceased to mention the origin of May Day in the United States and threw all of their support behind Labor Day. To be sure, individual unions affiliated with the AFL, especially those with socialist leadership and membership, continued to participate in May Day parades and meetings. But by 1905, the AFL made no references in its official publications to the Federation's role in founding May Day as a day of labor demonstration, or to the fact that May Day had originated in the United States. So far as the AFL was officially concerned, only Labor Day was a day to be celebrated by workers in the United States.[91]

Socialists and Wobblies Carry the Banner

In *The Worker*, then the Socialist Party of America's weekly published in New York City, Eugene V. Debs criticized the AFL for abandoning the celebration of May Day and urged radical organizations to continue the May Day tradition. In the May Day edition of April 27, 1907, Debs wrote in *The Worker*: "This is the first and only International Labor Day. It belongs to the working class and is dedicated to the revolution."[92]

From its founding convention in 1905, the Industrial Workers of the World (IWW) made it clear that it would celebrate May Day annually. On the eve of May Day, 1907, the *Industrial Union Bulletin*, official organ of the IWW, carried a front-page article entitled, "Meaning of the First of May." It argued: "Labor Day has completely lost its class character. The very fact that 'Labor Day' was legally, formally and officially established by the capitalist class itself, through its organized government, took the 'starch' out of it: destroyed its class character." On the other hand: "The First of May has not been disgraced, contaminated and blasphemed by capital's official sanction and approval, as has Labor Day. The capitalist class can never be a friend of May Day; it will ever be its enemy...."[93]

Pointing out that the "First of May, is dead and buried by its originators, the American Federation of Labor," the IWW pledged to take up the task of celebrating the true workers' holiday and to unite with all willing to join in the celebration.[94] It also pledged to honor the memory of the Haymarket martyrs, noting that while their voices are stilled by death, their memory is the grim nemesis of the rule of despotism and the sway of the boss."[95]

In 1911 the IWW initiated a campaign to line up the working class for the eight-hour day in a national demonstration on May 1, 1912. By July 1911, eight-hour day conferences and eight-hour leagues, under the sponsorship and leadership of the IWW, were formed in a number of cities, and thousands of eight-hour stickers were printed and distributed, reading:[96]

I
Won't Work
more
than 8 hours
after May 1st 1912
How about You
?

At its September 1911 convention, the IWW dropped the May 1, 1912, target date as unrealistic, but it never dropped the issue from its demands. Wobbly activitists, including Lucy Parsons,* used the eight-hour demand in unemployed organizing and in major IWW strikes.[97] At the same time, the IWW insisted that "the eight hour demand ... will not free the working class from the thraldom of capitalism. Labor's control of industries is the only panacea."[98]

May Day Members Grow

By May Day, 1911, the IWW claimed credit for the fact that the celebration of May 1 as its labor day "is beginning to spread among the working class of this country."[99] Actually, however, it was the Socialist Party of America together with groups of unions affiliated with the AFL that made the major contribution to keeping May Day alive in the United States. "With Parade and Mass Meetings in Rain, Socialists and Industrials [IWW] Observe May Day," proclaimed the *New York Herald* on May 2, 1909. "Hosts of workers Celebrate May Day," read the headline in the Socialist New York *Call.*[100] Women and children marched in their own trade sections, the children wearing ribbons with slogans in English, Russian or Yiddish, saying "Down with Slavery," "Abolish Child Labor."[101]

On April 28, 1910, the *New York Times* predicted that "50,000 union men and Socialists will parade down Fifth Avenue to Union Square on the occasion of the annual May Day parade. Delegations from the Central Federated Union and the American Federation of Labor will swell the line." The number of demonstrators on May 1, 1910, proved to be more than predicted, a major reason being that 20,000 women workers marched in the parade. "Yesterday's May Day pa-

---

*Lucy E. Parsons, the militant widow of Haymarket martyr Albert R. Parsons, was a founding member of the Industrial Workers of the World. (Philip S. Foner, *History of the Labor Movement in the United States* 4 [New York, 1965]:34, 36, 140, 437.)

rade," the *Times* reported, "will be remembered for the number of women marchers, more than a third of the 60,000 Socialist union men [sic] in line being of that sex. They represented the largest number of women ever taking part in a New York parade." The *Times* noted further that "the feature of the parade was the presence of 10,000 girls and young women of the Shirt Waist Makers' Union who had conducted the great 'Uprising of the 20,000' in 1909."* Finally, the *Times* pointed out that "nearly every labor organization was represented in the parade, which was held under the auspices of the Central Federation of Labor Unions affiliated with the American Federation of Labor, the United Hebrew Trades, and the Socialist Party of America."[102]

The following year the *New York Times* reported: "Fully 500,000 persons, mostly residents of the East Side, turned out yesterday afternoon to watch the annual Socialist and organized labor May Day parade. Forty-two locals marched. They carried banners reading: "We protest the kidnapping of McNamara";** "Protect Your Lives Through Your Organizations";*** "Capital Makes 0; Labor Makes Everything; Labor Enjoys 0."[103]

The *New York Times'* description of the 1913 May Day parade in New York City by the Socialist Party and the trade unions mentioned "hundreds of banners and placards boasting of strikes won in the last year, and denouncing in hundreds of red-lettered sandwich signs the capitalist system and the 'exploitation of labor.' " It continued:[104]

> Some 50,000 organized workers, men and women, wearing the bright red of socialism as the worldwide bond of labor—the girls dressed in white with red sashes and with red bands in their hats—marched through the streets of Manhattan yesterday to celebrate the 1st of May, the international holiday of workers. They ended in Union Square where a mass meeting was held at which eight-hour work-day resolutions were passed and Socialist speeches made.
>
> Similar demonstrations were held under the auspices of the Socialists in other cities throughout the United States.

*For the great strike of the waistmakers, see Philip S. Foner, *History of the Labor Movement in the United States* 5 (New York, 1980):226–240.

**The reference is to the illegal removal of the brothers John J. and James B. McNamara by detective William J. Burns from Indianapolis to Los Angeles to charge them with responsibility for the explosion on October 1, 1910 which destroyed a printing plant of the Los Angeles *Times*, killing twenty-one *Times* employees. (See Ibid., pp. 7–31.)

***The Triangle Fire occurred March 25, 1911, at the Triangle Shirtwaist Company in New York, during which 146 women workers died.

On May Day, 1914, the police attacked the Union Square rally of Socialists and trade unionists. The headlines in the *New York Times* the following day read: "Police Clubs. Women and Children Felled in Fight at Union Square May Day Rally." The reporter noted that "two little babies were crawling in the dust after the police attack, with their mother trying to crawl to them from a point ten feet away."[105]

On the eve of World War I (1913), May Day was celebrated for the first time in three Latin American countries: Mexico, Costa Rica, and Ecuador. May 1st was hailed in all three as the "Day of the Workers." In Costa Rica, all workers were invited by the committee of trade unions formed for the purpose, "without distinction of race, nationality, religion or political opinions to commemorate the First of May as a Day of Labor."[106]

Plakat der Sozialistischen Partei Italiens zum 1. Mai 1902

International May Day, 1917.

SOCIAL EVENING,

MASONIC HALL, JEPPE STREET,

JOHANNESBURG.

Chairman, ANDREW WATSON.

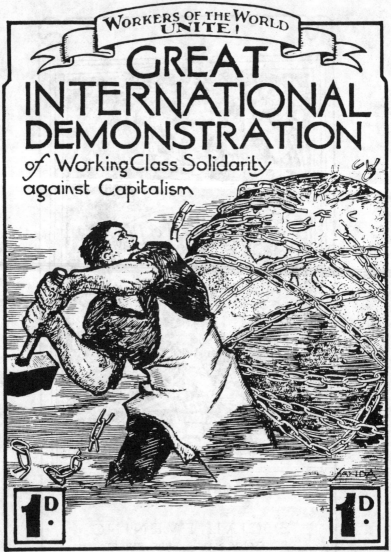

WORKERS OF THE WORLD UNITE!

GREAT INTERNATIONAL DEMONSTRATION
of Working Class Solidarity against Capitalism

1D. **1D.**

ALL LONDON FIRST OF MAY DEMONSTRATION COMMITTEE (1932)

Secretary—P. A. PALMER   Treasurer—G. P. KEMPTON   Chairman—J.R.SCOTT

PROCESSION from the THAMES EMBANKMENT

ASSEMBLE 1.30 p.m.   **LEAVE 2.0 p.m.**

Norfolk Street, Temple Station. *Brakes:* West Side. *Foot:* East Side; and proceed to **HYDE PARK** by way of Norfolk Street, Kingsway, Oxford Street. Marble Arch.

5

World War I to the Great Depression

In 1907, the Stuttgart Congress of the Second International resolved that if war did come, "the Socialists shall take measures to bring about its early termination and strive with all their power to use the economic and political crisis created by the war to arouse the masses politically and hasten the overthrow of capitalist rule." This policy was reaffirmed unanimously in 1912 at a conference in Basel, and was supposed to guide all participating Socialist parties.[1]

On the eve of World War I, May Day demonstrations throughout Europe and in the United States emphasized the importance of maintaining peace. "The working men of Berlin," went one report, "held 73 May Day meetings at which resolutions favoring disarmament in the interest of world peace was adopted. Perfect order was maintained."[2]

Betrayal by the Social Democrats

With the exception of those in Italy and Russia (and later in the United States), the various Socialist parties of the warring countries ignored the resolutions adopted at previous congresses when war was declared in August 1914. They yielded to the pressure of the ruling classes and to the demagogic description of their war aims. The Socialist leaders declared a truce in the class war and gave support to the bourgeois governments. Each justified the support of its ruling class in the war by invoking the necessity of defending its country against invaders. Of the 110 Socialist members in the German Reichstag, only Karl Liebknecht voted against the war and the war budget. In each belligerent country, only minorities of the Socialist leadership adhered to the Socialist position; the largest and most influential were the Bolsheviks in Russia.[3]

May Day, 1915, the first May Day after the outbreak of World War I, revealed the betrayal by the Social-Democratic leaders. The German Social Democracy called upon the workers to remain at work; the French Socialists in a special manifesto assured the authorities that they need not fear the first of May. In Spain and Switzerland, the Socialists held large demonstrations denouncing the war and militarism,[4] but neither of these two countries was involved in the war.

By mid-February 1916, 670,000 German soldiers had died and over one million were wounded. In this situation a series of letters signed "Spartacus" began to appear in Germany. They called for an immediate end to "the vile crime" of mass murder, and urged the soldiers of every nation to turn their guns against the exploiting classes. They also attacked the majority Socialist leaders of the German Social-Democratic Party. The leader of the "Spartakusbund" was Karl Liebknecht, and associated with him were Rosa Luxemburg, Clara Zetkin, Wilhelm Pieck, Leo Joyiches, Paul Levi, and a few other well known left-wing Socialists.[5]

In April 1916, the Spartakusbund distributed Karl Leibknecht's leaflet "On to May Day." He wrote:[6]

Comrades. For the second time May 1st occurs in the midst of bloody warfare—workers are the cannon fodder of imperialism.

Workers, comrades and women of the People.

Let not this second May Day of the world war pass by without a protest of international Socialists against the imperialist slaughter.

On the first of May we reach out a brotherly hand to the people in France, in Belgium, in Russia, in England, in Serbia, in the entire world.

Our enemies are not the French, Russian, or English people. They are the German junkers, German capitalists, and the German regime.

The Spartakusbund announced a mass meeting in the Potsdamer Platz in Berlin at 8:00 p.m. on May 1. Nearly 10,000 people jammed the Square to hear Liebknecht speak for peace, bread and freedom. When he said "Down with the war! Down with the government!" he was dragged from the platform by mounted police and troops and arrested.[7]

Liebknecht was tried for "attempted treason," "aggravated disobedience" and "contumacy to the authority of the state," found guilty, stripped of his Reichstag seat, dishonorably discharged from the Army, and given a two and a half year prison sentence. He appealed to a higher court, but as a result of his anti-war speech to the court, his sentence was increased to four years.[8]

Workers War Against War

The Majority Socialists had denounced Liebknecht's May Day demonstration, calling it a "grotesque" enterprise.[9] However, on May 1, 1916, workers in Barmen, Bremen, Dresden, Jena, Leipzig, Magdeburg, Stuttgart, Weimar and other German cities joined in protest against the imperialist slaughter.[10] The following year, May 1, 1917, half the workers in the Rhine provinces went on strike, as did the workers in the Krupp factories in Essen.[11]

The most widely celebrated May 1 was in Russia. May Day, 1917, was the first May Day after the February Revolution. While Russia still remained in the war, May Day demonstrators supported the Bolshevik's demand for peace. The special cable published in the *New York Times* described the May Day celebration:[12]

> All Petrograd is en fête today and business is at a complete standstill. Every means of conveyance is stopped, and it is even impossible to obtain any service whatever in the hotels, while the restaurants and cafe's are closed.
>
> The streets are filled with unending processions carrying banners with almost every kind of inscription such as "The Land and Will of the People," "Long Live the People," "Down with Militarism," "Long Live the International," "All Power to the Soviets," "Down with War." The capital inaugurated its first May Day fête without fear of opposition from any reactionary quarter. Over a million people participated in the parades. The Government had proclaimed the day a general holiday, and all the Governmental offices were closed.

In Berlin, Braunschweig, Dresden, Hannover, Leipzig, Magdeburg, and other cities in Germany protests against bread rationing began on April 16 and soon involved a half million workers. The Spartacus group distributed leaflets calling for strikes on May 1, 1917:[13]

> War against War! Up for the May 1st celebration.
>
> Women workers! Male workers! The last groans of our thousands of murdered brothers and sons, the sobs of the wasted women and children call us forcibly and imperiously to the red workers' May 1st demonstration, with the gleaming words: Down with the war! Up with people's brotherliness....
>
> The victory of our Russian brothers is our victory, it is a victory of the international proletariat . 27. a victory of international Socialism. It is a light pointing the way.... The Revolution in Russia has triumphed and its victory points the way for us....
>
> And now to the struggle, to the May Day celebration—to the workers' strikes in the factories.

May 1, 1918, was the first May Day after the Bolshevik Revolution, an event that gave new impetus and significance to the tradition of May Day. The Central Committee of the Russian Communist Party issued a May Day proclamation asserting that "Soviet Power Lives," and calling for unity against the imperialist war, for peace and brotherly unity of the workers of all nations. "After the victory over capitalism, we must rescue our people from hunger and unemployment."[14]

The first May Day demonstration in London since the start of World War I took place on May 5, 1918. It was called to celebrate the centenary of the birth of Karl Marx, but the authorities intervened. The London *Times* reported that a crowd which appeared to have reached "5,000 people assembled in Finsbury Park at half past 3 and grouped themselves around improvised stands. There were a few attempts to make impromptu speeches, but mounted police arrived and broke up the crowd."[15]

In the United States, May Day demonstrations were mainly devoted to preventing the entrance of the nation into the imperialist war. The *New York Times* described the 1916 May Day parade in New York as follows:[16]

One of the greatest May Day demonstrations of union workingmen and Socialists ever witnessed in the city was held yesterday. The masses turned out by the tens of thousands, either to march in the big parade or to line Fifth Avenue and other streets, and shout their sympathy to the marchers. Altogether it is probable that the unions and Socialist Party turned out more than 100,000 strong for the May Day parade.

The demonstrators carried banners denouncing militarism, and featuring such slogans as "We demand the immediate restoration of peace"; "Let those who preach war go to war." Speakers at Union Square emphasized that "the thinking workingmen of New York are not going to stand for war or militarism." Joseph D. Cannon, president of the Western Federation of Miners, told the huge audience:

We depend upon you workingmen to keep us out of war. If war is started and continues for any length of time, there will be a revolution against it.

Resolutions were adopted protesting against "any policy which may draw this country into war," the presence of American troops* in Mexico, and the use of the state militia against striking workers.[17]

*In March 1916, President Woodrow Wilson sent General John J. Pershing with U.S. troops into Mexico on a "punitive expedition" against Francisco "Pancho" Villa, who had raided U.S. territory. This was the second time Wilson had ordered an invasion of Mexico. In 1914 U.S. troops occupied Vera Cruz.

May Day was not abandoned when the United States declared war against Germany on April 6, 1917. In keeping with the anti-war resolution that the Socialist Party adopted at the Emergency St. Louis Convention early in April, some anti-war Socialists tried to utilize May Day to protest against the imperialist war. The largest May Day parade in the history of Cleveland was led on May 1, 1917, by Charles E. Ruthenberg, local secretary of the Socialist Party and a leading figure among left-wing Socialists. The demonstrators marched through the central area bearing banners that denounced the war and capitalism.[18]

In New York City the Socialist Party decided not to hold its annual parade, but instead settled for a mass meeting in Union Square, though a heavy downpour kept the meeting small. In a number of cities May Day demonstrations were cancelled. "Because of the war conditions," explained one paper, "the big celebrations of former years were not repeated in Chicago, Philadelphia, Pittsburgh, Toledo and Milwaukee."[19]

"May Day," the *New York Times* commented on May 1, 1918, "will find the nation's war work going forward without hindrance by a single individual strike of consequence." A May Day meeting scheduled for the Brooklyn Labor Lyceum was cancelled by the Trustees after the hall was filled. When the audience protested, the police broke up the gathering which then moved over to Socialist Party headquarters where Jim Larkin, the militant Irish Socialist addressed the meeting.[20] There were protests in a number of cities against the tremendous rise in the price of bread, and the protesters denounced brokers, speculators, and bankers who were making millions exporting wheat to the Allies.[21]

Frame-Ups and the "Red" Scare

May Day 1919 took place in the midst of a "red scare" in the United States, intensified on the eve of May Day by the discovery of bombs in the post offices said to be addressed to thirty-six wealthy individuals. The *Liberator*, a left-wing Socialist journal, charged that the so-called May Day bombs were "a frame-up by those who are interested in 'getting' the leaders of radicalism, and feel the need of a stronger public opinion before they can act." But A. Mitchell Palmer, Attorney-General of the United States, charged that the bombs were part of a "Bolshevik plot" to overthrow the government on May Day. "Reds Plan May Day Murders," blared the headlines in the nation's commercial press.[22]

Despite threats, American radicals and unionists staged rallies, held mass meetings, and conducted parades on May 1, 1919. In Boston the police attacked 1500 marchers in a parade sponsored by the Lettish Workmen's Association, and after a battle during which the police were aided by a mob of bystanders, one police officer was mortally stabbed and one civilian was wounded. Mobs then proceeded to demolish the Boston Socialist headquarters while vigilantes all over the city went on a rampage against Socialists. Ultimately 116 May Day paraders were arrested, charged with rioting and resisting the police. Fourteen were found guilty of disturbing the peace and sentenced to prison terms ranging from six to eighteen months. Not a single member of the mob was arrested.[23]

In Detroit, where 12,000 workers were on strike, the police stopped the workers from holding a parade. In Chicago the police also stopped a May Day demonstration. In New York no parade was permitted, but a May Day rally was held in Madison Square as a Tom Mooney protest meeting.* Signs around the Garden read: "We demand freedom for our Comrade Tom Mooney"; "We demand freedom for our Comrade Eugene V. Debs."[24]**

Headlines in the press on May 2, 1919, read: "Soldiers and Sailors Break Up Meetings in New York." The reference was to the attacks on the Russian People's House, and the offices of the New York *Call*, the Socialist Party daily, by 400 soldiers and sailors (aided by some civilians). The mob confiscated literature and smashed office furniture. At the Russian People's House the vigilantes forced the May Day gathering to sing the "Star Spangled Banner," and at the *Call's* office they broke up a May Day reception of 700 people, and drove them into the street with such violence that seventeen had to receive first aid.[25]

The anti-May Day rioting reached its peak in Cleveland. A peaceful parade, again led by Charles E. Ruthenberg, was halted by a mob led by an army lieutenant, who demanded that the soldier leading the parade drop his red flag. When the paraders refused, the lieutenant tore the flag from the soldier's hands. During the mob attack that followed, twenty Socialists were injured. Over 20,000 workers con-

---

*Thomas J. (Tom) Mooney and Warren K. Billings were framed in a bomb explosion incident during the 1916 Preparedness Day Parade in San Francisco. Mooney was sentenced to death and Billings to life imprisonment, but a series of labor protests in St. Petersburg, Russia played a role in the commuting of Mooney's sentence to life imprisonment. Despite ever-mounting evidence of their innocence, Mooney and Billings remained in prison for twenty more years.

**For opposing U.S. entrance into World War I, Eugene V. Debs was sentenced to twenty years in Federal prison.

tinued the parade to the Public Square where they were augmented by thousands more. Here the police and more vigilantes attacked several Socialist soldiers who refused to surrender the red flags they wore on the breasts of their uniforms. Five demonstrators were so severely beaten that they "required treatment by ambulance surgeons."[26]

The Socialist Party headquarters were then raided and completely wrecked by the mob of soldiers and civilians. By the time the raids were over, one person was killed, over fifty were wounded, and 106 Socialists were arrested and charged with responsibility for the riots. Not a single soldier or civilian vigilante was arrested.[27] The following report published in the *New York Times* on May 3, 1919, reveals the hysteria that was sweeping the nation:

> Federal troops with two machine-gun companies, equipped with motor trucks, were mobilized outside of Cleveland to suppress any disorder resulting from the Socialist May Day demonstration in the event the police proved incapable to cope with it.

Canadian workers were also on the march. On May Day of 1919, workers from Vancouver to Montreal, English- and French-speaking, celebrated in mass demonstrations. They hailed the Bolshevik Revolution and demanded higher pay, jobs for war veterans, an end to war measures and benefits for farmers. In addition, a several months' struggle in Winnipeg centered around a strike by metal workers turned into a general strike in May with 30,000 workers out on strike, including the city police. Winnipeg authorities were convinced they faced "revolution," but the main demands of the strike were the right to collective bargaining and the right to a living wage. The armed forces were called in to smash an essentially peaceful demonstration. Two workers were killed and thirty seriously wounded. Then a campaign of intimidation, arrests, trials and deportations took place aimed at weakening the working-class movement.[28]

Speaking in Petrograd on May 1, 1919 Lenin noted that "today not only in Red Moscow, in Red Petrograd, and in Budapest, but in all great proletarian centers, the workers are out in the street, marching, demonstrating their strength."[29] In Budapest, more than 90,000 workers demonstrated on May 1 under the red flag of the Hungarian Red Republic. Next door in the new Austrian Republic, under the leadership of the Socialists, Karl Reiner wrote in the "May Day Manifesto 1919": "A turning-point in history is here, the struggle for Democracy is ended—the work at Socialism begins."[30]

In Paris the call went out for a complete cessation of work on the

"First May Day of Peace." In spite of the rain and the government's prohibition of any meeting or procession, toward noon on May 1 a great crowd of working men and women flowed down toward the center of the city, heading for the Place de la Concorde where they tried to hold a meeting. But the entire area was cut off by troops who had been brought in during the night and early morning. At three o'clock the attempt was made to meet. One reporter wrote:[31]

A procession led by a youth carrying a Red Flag and demonstrators shouting "Vive la Russie," moved slowly down from the Madelene. As it crossed the Place de la Opera at the corner of the Chausee d' Anents, mounted Republican Guards cut them off and the police set about the task of breaking up the procession. They did so with great violence and, to the onlooker, with unnecessary brutality. More than one of the demonstrators were stunned by the kicks and truncheon blows they received. The procession was broken up.

Although one demonstrator was killed and 428 policemen injured during the attack,[32] the workers of Paris had displayed their power in the complete cessation of work on May Day. Socialist Deputy Marcel Cachin wrote in *Humanité*:[33]

The day was a magnificent demonstration of the power and discipline of the laboring classes, and was marred only by the brutality of the ferocious police. The responsibility for the disorders was entirely due to the provocation by the police, who were acting on orders from Premier Clemenceau. He alone is responsible.

The *New York Times*, however, was furious that in their May Day manifesto, the French workers had called for disarmament as well as for an eight-hour day. "What have the labor interests to do with that?" it asked angrily. "Is not this whole program purely Bolshevist radicalism. And why should the workingman concern himself with it as if it were a matter of his class interests?" The *Times* was also furious because the May Day demonstrators had signed cards reading: "I respectfully protest against the intervention in Russia."[34]*

May Day, 1919, was the first national republican holiday in Germany since the abdication of Kaiser Wilhelm. In its May Day manifesto, the Spartacus League in Munich welcomed the end of the Hohenzollern regime. But it noted: "The Hohenzollerns and their fellow-criminals were merely the figure heads of the international capitalists. The dominance of capitalism in Germany, as in France,

*All of the Allied nations, including the United States, had intervened militarily in Russia to overthrow the Bolshevik government.

in Russia, as in England, in Europe, as in America, was the true abettor of the world war." The manifesto warned of a counter-revolution, assisted by the Social Democrats, and called on the workers to arm themselves so as to be able to meet and defeat the troops of the counterrevolution who were already killing German revolutionary workers. "Rise up proletarians!" the Manifesto appealed. "Stand to arms! There is a world to conquer and a world to fight! It will be a fight to the finish!"[35]

As the manifesto warned, the troops of the counterrevolution supported by the right-wing Socialist government, killed hundreds of workers in Germany on May Day—a prelude to the murder of Karl Liebknecht and Rosa Luxemburg.[36]

May Day was celebrated in various parts of England by Socialist meetings, and in a number of cases by the cessation of work. The meeting in London's Hyde Park, preceded by a parade, was "attended by thousands of people, most of whom wore red ties, buttonholes, or rosettes." In Coventry the factories were shut down, the bakeries did not bake, and the tramway cars did not run. Forty thousand miners in Lancashire stopped work, and in the eight colliery counties in Scotland, miners were "on holiday." Under their new agreement, the Clyde dockers of Glasgow received a general holiday on May First. The only arrests in England on May Day were those of Sylvia Pankhurst and several of her followers when they attempted to force an entrance into the House of Commons on May Day to demand woman suffrage.[37]

"Dublin, like three-fourths of Ireland, has spent an absolutely idle day," was the report of May Day, 1919, in Ireland. "At the behest of the Irish Trades Congress and Labour Party, work of all kinds was suspended over the greater part of the country. Every shop in Dublin was closed and every factory and mill. There was no work at the docks and no steamers sailed and the theatres and picture houses were unopened. The only places in which business was transacted were the banks and Government offices, and only the threat of instant dismissal kept the civil servants and government employees at work."[38]

At meetings held all over Ireland resolutions were adopted demanding an international league of peoples as opposed to a league of governments,* repudiating the right of capitalists to exploit individuals for the purposes of profit; and declaring as just the de-

*The reference is to the League of Nations included as a clause in the Treaty of Versailles ending World War I.

mands of Irish workers for an improvement upon the standard of living that had prevailed in pre-war days. "A feature of the Labour-day procession in Southern Ireland," noted a reporter, "was the carrying of the Red Flag by the Transport Workers' Union."[39]

On May 1, 1919, May Day demonstrations by Socialists took place in Capetown and Johannesburg, South Africa. In its special May Day Paper, the official organ of the International Socialist League of South Africa voiced the feeling of hope caused by the victories of the Russian workers and peasants over their exploiters. Every year, it noted, "the import of May Day, International Labour Day, expands. Today the working class is at work on the liberation of all the exploited masses and oppressed races—for oppression is but a weapon of exploitation on every continent, of every colour and race.... This May Day is a day of greater rejoicing than ever before, since history and current events alike promise to the working-class movement a victory in our time—a victory when all men shall labour for the common good, and poverty, profit and oppression be unknown for evermore."

The 1919 demonstration in Johannesburg was huge. Workers downed tools and marched section by section behind their union banners to the meeting grounds where trade unionists and members of the International Socialist League joined hands to celebrate. The great weakness in the demonstration was the exclusion of African, Coloured and Indian workers.*

On the same May Day, F. A. Malan, the reactionary, racist Acting Premier, introduced a bill in Parliament calling for registration of aliens and deportation of all persons "participating in Bolshevik or other dangerous propaganda."[40]

In the fall of 1919 both the Communist Party and the Communist Labor Party were formed in the United States. On January 2, 1920, Attorney-General A. Mitchell Palmer launched a series of raids to round up alleged alien members of the Communist parties for deportation. In the course of the "Palmer Raids," over 6,000 men and

---

*The first May Day demonstration in South Africa was held in 1895. It was organized by the Johannesburg District Trades Council. Capetown held its first May Day celebration in 1906.

May Day demonstrations in South Africa were usually held under the auspices of the Social Democratic Federation. The Federation noted in its report of the 1915 meeting: "It was a grand meeting. The audience of all colours showed a deep interest in the speeches." The speeches called on the workers of South Africa to "fight for unity of all peoples and the abolition of capitalist exploitation, brutality, and bloodshed." (E. R. Braverman, "The Story of May Day in South Africa," *New Age*, South Africa, April 26, 1956, p.4.)

women were arrested by federal agents, and 556 aliens, though convicted of no crimes, were deported.[41]

On the eve of May Day, 1920, Palmer warned of a nationwide plot by Communists to assassinate national and state officials, and establish a Soviet America. "City Under Guard Against Red Plot Threatened Today in Interest of Soviet Russia," was the headline in the *New York Times* of May 1, 1920. But on May 2, the *Times* reported that "All Demonstrations are Peaceful."[42]

A "significant feature" of the May Day demonstration in London was the prominent part taken by the cooperative movement. A large number of cooperative societies closed their shops and factories for May Day in order that their workers might join in the procession. Previously the cooperative movement had taken only a small part in May Day demonstrations.[43]

The procession, headed by a contingent of about 500 of the National Union of Ex-Service Men, "took more than an hour to pass a given point" and was watched "by enormous crowds." "The hundreds of gaily-colored banners represented almost every trade union." The banner of the National Federation of the Building Operatives read "44 no more" in support of their demand for a shorter working week. Another said: "Solidarity of Labour Means Permanent Peace." On the way to Hyde Park, the procession made a detour to the Polish Legation where a protest was lodged against the Polish offensive in the Soviet Union. Cries of "Long Live Soviet Russia" were raised by the demonstrators.[44]*

The resolution adopted simultaneously at twelve platforms in Hyde Park began:

> This mass meeting of London workers sends fraternal greetings to their trade union, cooperative and Socialist comrades throughout the world, who this day assemble to demonstrate their solidarity, and their determination to substitute an International Cooperative Commonwealth for the present capitalist and landlord system, which is responsible for innumerable social problems and hardships.

The resolution demanded "immediate effective attention" to the solution of "some of the pressing problems" such as:

> Adequate provision for housing and means of transit; Amnesty to political and military prisoners: Employment for able-bodied adults on

*At the May 1, 1923, demonstration in London's Hyde Park one of the resolutions passed demanded that strong representation be made "to the Imperialist Japanese government" to withdraw her troops "without delay from the island of Sakhalan which belongs to Russia." (London *Times*, May 2, 1923.)

work useful to the community; Endowment for motherhood; Equal pay
for men and women: Full maintenance for workers disabled in the war
and their dependants; Full compensation for workers disabled in the
war, and their dependents; Full compensation for all workers injured
in industry, and support for widows, orphans, and the infirm; The
abolition of the Aliens Restriction Act; The abolition of the present
charitable system; and The adoption of state support and control of
the blind.

The resolution hailed "with enthusiasm the success of the Russian
Soviet government, and calls on workers in all countries to refuse
to provide munitions of war or the means of intervention by British
and other capitalist Governments, and pledges itself to use its efforts
to force those Governments to conclude peace with Soviet Russia
on the basis of no annexation, no indemnities, and no interference
in Russian internal affairs." It also demanded "the withdrawal of
British troops from Ireland, and proclaims the right of the Irish
people to choose their own form of Government." It demanded "that
all questions of peace or war must rest ultimately with the workers."
Finally, the resolution demanded "full recognition and support of
the industrial cooperative movement as a method of ensuring do-
mestic supplies free from profiteering," and denounced the proposal
to impose an income tax on the savings secured by cooperative
mutual trading societies.[45]
Similar resolutions were adopted at May Day rallies throughout
England and Scotland.[46] A feature of the demonstrations in many
parts of England was the presence of agricultural laborers and farm
hands. "In some cases," one reporter wrote, "the farmers placed
their horses and wagons at the disposal of the Labourers' Union."[47]
In France, the railwaymen announced a general strike for May
Day, and the Confederation Generale du Travail (CGT) ordered out
the seamen and dockers as a proof of their "entire sympathy with
and active support of the railwaymen."[48] In an appeal to the workers
of Paris, the CGT urged them to avoid conflicts with the police and
troops on May Day: "Do not reply to provocation. No street demonstrations; no provocations; that is the watchword we give our
workers." Nevertheless, there were several clashes in Paris between
May Day demonstrators and the troops and police. The day began
peacefully but the police and the Republican Guards attacked the
demonstrators, the latter using sabres. Three of the demonstrators
were killed.[49]
School children were among the May Day demonstrators in Berlin.
They carried banners bearing mottoes reading: "We, too, strike on
May 1"; and "We want regular schools." The newly organized Com-

munist Party of Germany (KPD) marched with banners reading: "Hands Off the German Revolution"; "Hands Off Red Russia"; "Unity with Red Russia"; "Long Live the Third International";* "Long Live the World Revolution."[50]

May 1, 1920, saw the first May Day demonstrations in China. Organized by the Communist Party, they occurred in Shanghai, Tientsin, Canton and other industrial centers.[51] In Japan, the first May Day occurred on May 2, 1920. A group of trade union delegates in Tokyo who met in mid-April decided that since May 1 would fall on a Saturday, a work day for the Japanese, it would not bring a large response. It was decided to hold the demonstration on Sunday, May 2, and police permission was secured.

On May 2 workers gathered in front of their own union offices in Tokyo and marched quietly toward Ueno Park. When several workers marched in with a flag on which was inscribed in red lettering the slogan: "Death or Freedom," the police quickly seized the flag. A skirmish followed that was quieted down by the chairman of the meeting. After several speeches, the following declaration was read:

> Here have we held the first May Day in Japan. May Day is a celebration, indeed, but more importantly, it is the assertion of each worker's consciousness of himself as a disciplined, dependable and responsible human being. Only workers can understand the full impact and absorb the full joy of this day. We, here and now, supported by workers throughout the world, hereby proclaim liberty for the working classes and freedom for all people.
>
> This first May Day in Japan, we announce the following declarations:
> 1. To abolish Article 17 of the Security Police Act
> 2. To prevent unemployment
> 3. To establish the Minimum Wage Act.

The assembly unanimously adopted these three proposals as resolutions. Other resolutions then followed calling for an 8-hour work shift, the immediate withdrawal of Japanese troops from Siberia, and the introduction of public education. All were unanimously adopted.

At 3:30 p.m., the whistle blew to signal the end of the speeches and chairman Bunju Suzuki made the following closing remark:

> Although we held the first May Day on a Sunday, any day next year would do. If May 1st should fall on a work day, let's call it a day off and celebrate May Day.

*The Third International, or Communist International, was organized in Moscow in March 1919 under the auspices of the Bolsheviks.

And now, I would like to seal this address by relaying Marx's eternal words to you: "Workers of the world, unite!"[52]

The International Federation of Trade Unions (IFTU) which had disbanded during the war, reorganized in 1920. On the eve of May Day 1921, the Amsterdam Bureau of the Federation issued an appeal to the workers of the world, which was to serve as the program for the members of the twenty-four national union organizations affiliated with the IFTU.[53]

1921: Arrests on May Day Eve

On the eve of May Day, 1921, the Bomb Squad of the New York police and agents of the U.S. Department of Justice raided the headquarters of the Communist Party of America and arrested several leaders. On May Day, the bomb squad raided meetings of the Communist Party. The actions were justified on the grounds that the police had received information "which indicated that communists, extreme anarchists, and the Left Wing element of the Socialist Party were planning violent demonstrations at which they would call for the overthrow of the government."[54]

Men and women were arrested for distributing circulars and charged with criminal anarchy. The circulars, signed "The Central Executive Committee of the Communist Party of America," were published in the press. One read in part:[55]

> Working men of America, the bosses, the capitalistic class, are organized to crush you. They have openly declared they will smash your unions, reduce your wages and level you to the condition of serfs.... All the machinery of the United States is used against the workers for the benefit of the capitalistic class.
>
> Let us answer on May Day. Let us prepare for the revolution, as you are coming face to face with poverty and oppression.

May 1, 1921, saw New York harbor tied up by a strike of 40,000 seamen and firemen and 6,000 marine engineers. The printers struck in San Francisco, Denver, Salt Lake City, New Orleans; Halifax, Nova Scotia; and St. John's, Newfoundland. By May 2 the printers were in a nationwide strike for the eight-hour day. Chicago had a May Day parade for the first time in many years. Twenty thousand workers marched, while hundreds of extra police were put on duty.[56]

In London, 100,000 were at the Hyde Park demonstration. In Warsaw soldiers clashed with demonstrators, especially attacking contingents of Jewish Socialists. There were reports of 500 casualties.

In Rome the communists and fascists fought, and two deaths resulted. In Mayence, Germany, 20,000 workingmen paraded, many carrying banners proclaiming: "Whether the German or the French occupy the Ruhr it will always be owned by the bourgeoisie." May Day meetings in Tokyo, Yokohama, Osaka, and Kobe passed resolutions for the eight-hour day, the extension of the franchise to Japanese workers, and assistance for the unemployed. Banners at the meetings carried slogans reading: "From Slavery to Emancipation"; "Revolution is Near at Hand."[57]

Fear in the Hearts of Capitalists

The Metropolitan Opera House in New York City was crowded on May Day, 1925. "Instead of high-priced stars singing operatic scores, radical garment workers raised their voices in the 'Internationale,'" wrote the reporter for the *New York Times*. "The opera house was jammed as full as when Caruso used to sing."[58] Copies of the special May Day edition of the *Daily Worker*, organ of the Workers' (Communist) Party of America, were distributed featuring a statement by Charles E. Ruthenberg, general secretary of the Party:

> May Day—the day which inspires fear in the hearts of capitalists and hope in the workers—the workers the world over—will find the Communist movement this year stronger in the U.S. than at any time in its history.... The road is clear for greater achievements, and in the United States as elsewhere in the world the future belongs to communism.

The resolution adopted by the meeting began: "These May Day gatherings are so many warnings that the day of reckoning with the capitalist regime is near at hand." It went on to declare a "determination to fight the open-shop, child labor, and the Dawes Plan,* which would further enslave Germany's toiling millions, and to fight for the amalgamation of all workers' organizations into one world body. We declare our intention further to fight for the recognition of Soviet Russia."[59]

"Drastic steps to prevent a Communistic outbreak tomorrow, the International Labor Day, are being taken by police and military authorities all over Europe," was a report published on the eve of May Day, 1925, in France.[60] The French government issued orders against holding any demonstration, took measures to have Paris

---

*The Dawes Plan was a plan for German reparations payments recommended in 1924 by a committee headed by banker Charles G. Dawes.

fully policed, and even had the military ready. After protests by Socialists, Communists, and the trade unions, the government allowed meetings outside the city limits.[61]

In London the annual demonstration was organized by the First of May Celebration Committee of the Workers' Movement. Demonstrators carried banners reading: "Marx and Lenin Lead Us"; "Long Live Soviet Russia"; "Free India"; "British Empire Exhibit, Our Poverty is Part of It." The resolutions welcomed the recent steps taken by the British Trade Union Congress to secure unity between the British and Soviet trade unions, and to secure the admission of the Russian workers into the International Federation of Trades Unions.[62]

The 1926 May Day manifesto of the IFTU called on the working class to demand "the universal establishment of the eight-hour day, the recognition of the workers' right to a share in industrial control, and a true and lasting world peace:"[63]

Let each do what he can toward the attainment of these great aims and the founding of a new world. Let each do what he can to enlighten his comrades and give them a deeper sense of the historic mission of the working class—the emancipation of the world from the yoke of capitalism.
Long live international labor!
Long live international peace and solidarity!

May Day, 1926, in England took place as plans were under way for a general strike in support of the great British miners' strike. Contingents from the Labor Party, from the cooperative societies, the trade unions, the Independent Labour Party, and the Communist Party took part in the London May Day demonstration. "It was generally agreed," noted the London *Times*, "among the organizers that the crowd was one of the largest which had ever attended a Labour Day demonstration in London."[64] Mr. Saklatvala, M.P., speaking from the wagon of the Young Communist League, and to loud applause, said the government should take over the mines. Resolutions supporting a general strike were adopted.[65]

In Glasgow, "fully 20,000 persons took part in the procession." "The duty of the Government," said Wheatley, M.P., "is to take from the super-rich part of their super-wealth, and use that to settle the mining trouble.... The miners refuse to starve and the workers generally will support them."[66]

The workers did, and the General Strike began soon after May Day. It did not succeed, however, and the miners continued to hold out after it was ended. But they finally returned, defeated, in November 1926 after holding out for seven months.[67]

At the May Day celebration of the Workers' (Communist) Party at Cooper Union on May 1, 1926, Charles E. Ruthenberg discussed the strikes of textile and needle trades' workers in the United States, and then the impending general strike in England. A strike of 5,000,000 workers in England, he said, was not revolution, "but close to the brink." He predicted that the time would come "when capitalist governments would be done away with and socialist societies would take their place throughout the world.[68]

In a May Day speech to a meeting at New York's Manhattan Center of the Amalgamated Clothing Workers Sidney Hillman, ACW president, noted that contrary to the general impression that May Day as a workers' holiday was imported from Europe, the reverse was the case. He explained that in 1884 and 1885, the Federation of Organized Trades and Labor Unions, out of which emerged the American Federation of Labor, had set May 1, 1886, as the day on which U.S. workers should demonstrate for the eight-hour day.[69]

A concert by the New York Symphony Orchestra, under the auspices of the Italian Newspaper *Il Nuovo Mondo*, was turned into a May Day rally for the Passaic textile strikers, and a denunciation of Benito Mussolini and his fascist regime in Italy. During the intermission Elizabeth Gurley Flynn, the IWW's "Rebel Girl," marched onto the stage with a group of strikers' children and made an appeal for the strikers' families. "Her words were punctuated by the tinkle of coins in metal receptacles passed among the audience." After the concert, a meeting heard C. E. Ervin declare that "Mussolini was the greatest scoundrel unhung in the world."[70]

In 1923 the *New York Times* had reported from Italy that the fascists suppressed "the old Labor Day on May 1 and shifted the day forward by ten days, making it coincident with the birthday of Rome on April 21, which has been declared a national holiday." The Communists and Socialists, it added, had objected to this desecration of May Day, and attempted to hold demonstrations on the first of May as in the past, but they were attacked by police.[71]

On May 1, 1926, workers were forced to remain at work in Mussolini's Italy and elaborate police measures were taken to prevent any May Day demonstration. A number of workers in Turin, Milan, and other industrial centers remained away from work but were arrested when they tried to demonstrate. "One group of Communists, including Deputy Bendini, was rounded up in Rome and arrested," was the report in the press.[72] The day did not pass without bloodshed in Italy: four demonstrators were killed and thirty wounded.[73]

From China to Boston

The May Day Manifesto of the Bureau of the Social and Labor International for 1927 urged organized labor the world over to demand the immediate withdrawal of foreign troops and warships from China as a feature of the observance of May Day:[74]

> What is happening in China is the beginning of the great mutiny of the last great reserve army of capitalism.... The struggle of the Chinese people for complete self-determination fills with hopes of freedom the souls of the oppressed peoples of all colors and shows the imperialists of all countries that the epoch of colonial exploitation is coming to an end....
>
> And, therefore, on this 1st of May, we demonstrate again for the immediate recall of the foreign troops and warships from China.

The May Day meeting of the Workers' (Communist) Party in New York called for recall of foreign troops from China and the removal of U.S. marines from Nicaragua. It demanded that "China, Nicaragua, and Mexico be left alone." However, the main emphasis was on the impending execution of Sacco and Vanzetti for a crime they had not committed. The meeting demanded that "the death sentence of two innocent men" be rescinded.[75]*

In Boston, the May Day meeting sent greetings "and expressions of love and solidarity to you, Sacco and Vanzetti. We admire your courageous stand. We shall not rest content until you are free."[76] Throughout the United States, at May Day meetings sponsored by Communists and Socialists, the demands were for the release of Sacco and Vanzetti, "Hands Off China," "Non-Intervention in Mexico and Nicaragua," and "Down with Fascism."[77]

Twenty-five thousand marched through Mexico City to be greeted

---

*Niccola Sacco and Bartolomeo Vanzetti, Italian-American anarchists, were arrested in 1921 and charged with the murder of two employees of a shoe factory in South Braintree more than a year before. In a trial featured by anti-radical and anti-foreign hysteria, Sacco and Vanzetti were found guilty on purely circumstantial evidence and sentenced to death by electrocution. The Massachusetts supreme court and the U.S. Supreme Court refused to intervene. Despite worldwide protests and nationwide demonstrations in the United States, Sacco and Vanzetti were executed on August 22, 1927.

by President Calles and his Cabinet. "At noon, the marchers observed five minutes of silence in honor of the labor leaders who lost their lives in Chicago in the disturbances of 1886."[78]

In Berlin the traditional May Day demonstration in the Lustgarten was organized by the trade unions and not by the Socialist or Communist Party in order to create a unified demonstration. The political parties held their separate meetings in various parts of the city during the afternoon. After their meeting, the Communists led a march to the American Embassy to demand the release of Sacco and Vanzetti.[79]

The National Socialist Fascists held a "meeting" indoors at which Adolf Hitler spoke for the first time. Although the Nazi leader was still forbidden to speak in public in Prussia because of his part in the Munich "beerhall putsch" of November, 1923, he was allowed by the Weimar government to address his followers in private. But in Essen, Dartmund, Duisburg, and other German cities, demonstrators carried banners proclaiming: "Down with the Fascist murder gang"; "Long live the Chinese Revolution"; "Prepare for battle against the reactionary Steel Helmets."[80]

May Day was celebrated in the northeast part of Paris, and the prohibition of street processions by the Minister of the Interior compelled the demonstrators to go to the meeting in small parties.

Some 15,000 demonstrators in Tokyo, 2,000 of whom were women (mainly textile workers), assembled in Shiba Park and marched five miles across the city to Uyeno Park where speeches were delivered and resolutions adopted. The banners carried by the demonstrators bore such slogans as "We Want the Eight-Hour Day"; "Protect the Unemployed"; "Down with Unjust Laws." The resolutions demanded an eight-hour day, no intervention in China, compensation for day laborers injured at work, and formation of an all-Japan labor union.[81]

In China the reactionary Chiang Kai-shek, head of the Kuomintang government recently established in Nanking, prohibited the holding of May Day demonstrations, and execution of Communists by his henchmen continued even on May Day. But the trade unions, led by Communists, managed to distribute handbills in Hankow on May Day appealing to U.S. and British sailors to refuse to fire on Chinese: "You sailors on the warships come from the working class and should join us in union demands. Although your warships threaten the lives of our people, we workers and peasants greet you as class brothers. Would you kill us for this?"[82]

The May Day, 1927, parade in Moscow's Red Square was widely reported. The Moscow correspondent of the *New York Times* emphasized that the workers in the parade "were much better dressed," than previously, a sign of increasing prosperity in the Soviet Union.[83]

> Other striking characteristics of the tramping hosts were the high spirits and magnificent physique of Russia's youthful athletes of both sexes, who each year are playing a more important part in the civic festivals as well as in Communist life.
>
> This symbolizes one of the most profound changes in Russian life since the revolution. Before the war all Russia possessed only 30,000 organized athletes. Now in Moscow alone, the "non-party volunteer sports circles" comprise 60,000, the All-Russian Federation, 800,000, and the All-Union, 1,000,000 athletes in regular training.
>
> And more than 20 percent of these athletes are girls.

May 1, 1927, marked the first time May Day was officially observed in India. Unofficially there had been some small observation of May Day in India in 1923 and 1926. In 1925 the Indian sailors in the East End of London participated in the May Day meeting in Hyde Park. In response to an appeal from the All-India Trade Union Congress at its Delhi session in 1927 asking all its provincial units to observe May Day, there were demonstrations in Calcutta, Madras and Bombay. The Bombay meeting demanded that the eight-hour working day be fixed by law.[84] (The All-India Trade Union Congress, the first organized body of the Indian working class on an all-India basis, was founded in 1920.)

Walter Duranty, the famous correspondent of the *New York Times* in the Soviet Union, was deeply moved by the May Day demonstration of 1928 in Red Square:[85]

> Today's scene in Red Square was an astounding demonstration of the might of the armed proletariat. This was what was intended. For the First of May in Soviet Russia is not just Labor Day as it is elsewhere in Europe, but it is the day of Labour victorious to serve as an example and as an encouragement to the revolutionary spirit throughout the world.

Identical May Day appeals were published in 1928 in the German Socialist *Vorwarts* and the Communist *Rote Fahne*. In response members of both parties gathered together on the Treptow sports ground for the demonstration in Berlin. "The Socialists and Communists sank their differences in honour of the 'festival of labour,'" wrote the reporter for the London *Times*.[86]

Execution of Communists continued in China under Chiang Kai-shek on May Day, 1928. "In Shanghai," went a report in the press, "the execution of two alleged Communist women whom the French recently handed over to the Chinese authorities marked the day. The spectacle acted as a public warning."[87]

Circulars urging school children to join an "Out of School on May Day" movement were distributed at the public schools of New York City on April 30, 1928, by representatives of the Young Workers (Communist) League, the Young Pioneers of America, and the Children's May Day Conference. The children were also urged to attend the Madison Square Garden meeting of the Workers (Communist) Party in the afternoon of May Day.[88]

Since 1916, the New York police had banned a May Day parade, forcing Socialists and Communists to hold meetings without a procession to celebrate the holiday.

On the eve of May Day, 1928, the New York Council of the Unemployed announced plans to hold a demonstration in Union Square, and then march to the meeting in Madison Square Garden. But the police insisted on retaining the ban on parades. Chief Inspector Lahey told the press that "any attempt at a parade would be broken."[89]

May 1, 1929: "Made in America"

Permission for a parade was finally granted in 1929 by Police Commissioner Grover Whalen, soon to become notorious for leading the police in brutal attacks on the unemployed. A condition accompanied the permission. The parade was to be orderly; no "incendiary placards" were to be displayed, and an American flag was to be carried in the march. The conditions were accepted by the Workers' (Communist) Party, and for the first time since 1916, New York City witnessed a May Day parade. To celebrate the special occasion, the *Daily Worker* published the following poem by Henry George Weiss:[90]

MARCH TODAY

May Day!
Labor's Day!
Our day!
Made in America!
As American as the Fourth of July
And the Declaration of Independence.
Turned out of the crucible

Of the suffering
Of working men and women. . . .

Bolshevik Russia didn't give May Day to the
  American working class,
But the American working class gave May Day
  to the revolutionary workers of the world—
Gave the world May Day

O American workers
Red, white, yellow, black,
Come on, lift up your heads
Throw down your tools,

To hell with the boss
To hell with the factory whistle!
This is Labor Day, our day made in America—
  March!

Ten thousand demonstrators, including a large contingent of school children, marched from Union Square to Astor Place, Broadway, Waverly Place and back to Union Square for the May Day meeting. Heavy rain failed to diminish the spirit of the demonstrators. The police confiscated several red flags and some banners attacking the brutality of President Machado of Cuba and Dictator Primo de Rivera of Spain.[91]

In London May Day was celebrated with a one-day strike of women tailors. In Vienna, to mark the tenth anniversary of the formation of the Socialist government, the biggest Vienna May Day celebration ever took place.[92] In Mexico City the demonstration was referred to as "the annual demonstration glorifying the memory of those who were killed in Chicago in 1887," indicating how important a role in Mexico's May Day was played by the Haymarket martyrs.[93]

Demonstrations were forbidden in Greece, Bulgaria, Rumania, Hungary, Yugoslavia, Lithuania, and Czechoslovakia. In Paris the police arrested large numbers of people suspected of planning May Day demonstrations, and scores of foreigners were seized and summarily expelled from the country. Over 2,500 Communists were arrested, including two Communist deputies and the secretary of the CGT. All together 3,500 were arrested in Paris on May Day, 1928.[94]

In Berlin, open-air demonstrations were prohibited by the Socialist Chief of Police. The Socialist trade unions complied and held their May Day celebration "in orderly fashion under strong police protection in some 40 halls distributed over Berlin." The Communists, however, defied the ban and went ahead with holding open-air demonstrations. The police brutally attacked the demonstrators, and, firing into the crowds, killed between eight and thirty-one demonstrators, wounding hundreds—seventy seriously. Twelve hundred workers were arrested. "The Communists seemed determined to have their May Day martyrs," sneered the London *Times*.[95]

The Communist Party of New York called a protest meeting attended by 5,000 workers in Union Square to voice indignation against the murder of the May Day demonstrators by the " 'socialist-led' police of Berlin." Protest meetings were also held in a number of Soviet cities, and on the day of the burial of the slain Berlin workers, all activity ceased for a moment in Kharkov, flags were lowered to half mast, and sirens sounded.[96]

Twenty thousand Cuban workers, led by the illegal Communist Party, filled the "Nuevo Fronto" stadium in Havana on May Day, 1929. Pouring out of the stadium, 8,000 marched to the harbor where they filled boats to take them across the Bay to the suburb of Regla. There 3,000 workers joined the demonstration in a march to "Lenin's Tree." The tree had been planted immediately after the victorious Bolshevik Revolution, and it was an annual custom for workers from Havana to gather on May Day at the tree to pay tribute to the leader of the October Revolution.

This May Day a battle broke out between the police, aided by mounted soldiers, and the demonstrators. One worker was killed immediately and eighteen, including two women, were wounded, one of whom died later. Three policemen were also wounded. The following day, thousands of workers followed the coffins of the murdered demonstrators, Rudolfo Perez and Juan Monteigo, to the cemetery. Among the dozens of floral wreaths covering the coffins was one with the inscription: "As a reply to those sacrificed to the cause, the proletariat will fortify its revolutionary ranks."[97]

Red Square, Moscow, 1934. Photo is of Ernst Thaelman, German Communist leader jailed by the Nazis. Sign in foreground demands his freedom.

Section of May Day parade, London, 1934

Section of 1936 New York City May Day parade.

6

The Depression Through World War II (1929–1945)

"May Day Finds Labor Well Off in America," was a headline in the *New York Times* of May 2, 1926. According to the *Times*, employment was stable, wages were high and industrial peace general throughout the United States with radicalism showing little strength. Small wonder it concluded that "the traditional mark of May Day in Europe faded in the United States." Two years later, the *Times* repeated this analysis, this time adding that even "the condition of the workers in Western Europe" was improving and becoming close to that in the United States. (On the other hand, there was "no improvement" in working class conditions in the Soviet Union.) "At the present moment the rate of unemployment in France is down to zero. In Germany it has been sharply declining, in Great Britain it has been going down though more slowly, whereas unemployment in Soviet Russia is by far the highest in the world. Similar would be the comparison of wages in relation to prices, housing, and educational opportunities."[1]

It was not long before the *Times* would have to eat its words. In the early months of 1929, with the economy supposedly flourishing as never before, unemployment rose sharply in the United States. Over 300,000 Black workers, about one-fifth of all Black industrial workers, had already been thrown out of work.[2]

After the stock market crash of October 1929, the number of unemployed in the United States and Europe began to mount rapidly. U.S. unemployment rose from three million to approximately fifteen million in 1933, with many millions working part time. Wages dropped 45 percent and the percentage of the U.S. population living at or below the bare subsistence level rose from 40 percent in 1929 (the year of greatest prosperity) to 75 percent in 1932.

In Germany thirty-five million were unemployed in 1932, and more millions were working part time. As Clara Zetkin pointed out, May Day during the Great Depression was a "Hunger-May." The same conditions prevailed throughout the entire capitalist world.[3]

Meanwhile, the Soviet Union forged ahead. As the capitalist countries sank in an ever-deepening economic crisis, the Five Year Plan of Reconstruction in the Soviet Union surpassed the most optimistic forecasts for it. Not only was there no unemployment in the first Socialist country, but a shortage of labor brought unemployed workers from the United States and Europe to the Soviet Union.[4]

Hunger—and Fightback

In 1932, only one-quarter of the unemployed in the United States were receiving any form of relief. In New York City, families lucky enough to get relief obtained an average grant of $2.39 per week; in most places people got only a little food.[5] The government gave no aid; President Herbert Hoover kept assuring the people that "Prosperity is just around the corner."[6] Meanwhile, the unemployed could starve.

The unemployed, Black and white, refused to starve. They joined forces in a militant struggle for work, mostly under the leadership of both the Trade Union Unity League, formed in 1929 with William Z. Foster as secretary, and the Communist Party. The TUUL and the Communist Party began early in the Great Depression to organize the jobless into Councils of the Unemployed, later known as Unemployed Councils. From the outset, the TUUL and the CP demanded that "all unemployed shall be entitled to unemployed benefits sufficient to secure the maintenance of their families and dependents during the whole period of unemployment."[7]

March 6, 1930, was designated as International Unemployment Day by Communist parties in capitalist countries throughout the world. Under the slogan "Starve or Fight," the Unemployed Councils in the United States issued a call for a national demonstration. Hundreds of thousands of unemployed in some thirty cities and towns demonstrated in the largest series of unemployed protests in U.S. history.[8]

Violent clashes took place between police and demonstrators in a number of cities, especially in New York City's Union Square, where between 60,000 and 100,000 were brutally attacked by police acting on the orders of police Commissioner Grover Whalen. During the police attacks, William Z. Foster, Robert Minor and other Communist leaders were arrested. They were later sentenced to six months' prison terms.[9]

In a joint May Day Manifesto, the Trade Union Unity League and the Communist Party declared:[10]

> On May Day, unemployed and employed workers of the United States must demonstrate shoulder to shoulder with the workers of all countries for unemployment relief, unemployment social insurance, for the Defense of the Soviet Union and against imperialist war. Make May Day 1930 the largest symbol of the entire class....
>
> Fight for social insurance! Fight for work or wages! Against fascist terror! Unity of employed and unemployed workers! Fight against wage cuts! Build Unemployed Councils!

One thousand police, with machine guns and tear gas ready, were on duty at Union Square for the May Day demonstration. But the workers were not intimidated. "More than 100,000 persons participated in May Day demonstrations in Union Square," the press reported, "while machine guns appeared on the top of low buildings and their muzzles tilted downward to the Square." Posters carried by the demonstrators protested the continued detention of Foster and other Communist leaders.[11] The march proceeded from the lower East Side of New York to Union Square, the first contingents being made up of women, girls, and small children. "Wearing red sashes, red neckties, red hats and red scarves," wrote a reporter, "the paraders made a vivid spectacle as they moved slowly around the square, singing as they walked."[12]

"The crowd was so dense that one could move only by inches," but as a result of widespread protests, there was no repetition "of the violent scenes which marked the demonstration on March 6."[13]

In Chicago, following a parade, Lucy Parsons delivered the principal speech at the May Day rally; in Philadelphia, a demonstration was held in Independence Square.[14]

The Workers Unity League in Canada had a program similar to that of the TUUL in the USA in order to meet similar problems. On March 6, 1930, 20,000 unemployed workers in Montreal and 15,000 in Toronto demonstrated for jobs or unemployment insurance. Other mass actions took place in Edmonton, Winnipeg, Vancouver and Ft. William (Thunder Bay). The May Day demonstrations in Canada were the largest in Canada's history up to that time. Approximately 80,000 workers took part across the country.[15]

For two to three weeks before May Day, "Hunger marchers" had been converging on London to take part in the demonstration. Unemployed men and women from the industrial districts took to the road. They joined the Communists in the procession to Hyde Park, carrying banners reading, "Down with the Starvation Labour Government." Workers sold copies of the May Day issue of the *Daily Worker*, organ of the Communist Party, which appeared in an enlarged form. Two blank spaces on the front page bore the words "Censored by printer."[16]

On the eve of May Day, the Paris police raided the offices of *L'Humanité* and seized the May Day edition. During the day the police detained about 800 people, ninety of them foreigners "who will automatically be deported," the press reported. The Mayor was arrested while trying to organize a May Day demonstration at Denes, the Communist stronghold in the suburbs. Also arrested were the Communist Deputy and several members of the Municipal Council.[17]

Fifty persons were injured in Madrid when 10,000 May Day demonstrators were attacked by the Civil Guard and the police as they shouted, "Death to the King," "Long Live the Republic." On the eve of May Day, fifty Communists were arrested in Sofia, and every Communist leader in Bucharest was arrested. They were released on May 2.[18]

In Sydney, Australia, the police broke up a May Day procession, arresting seventeen. In Shanghai, police and foreign troops joined together to prevent demonstrations. Six thousand workers demonstrated on May Day in Tel Aviv, Palestine.[19]

A dispatch from Lima, Peru, dated April 30, read: "Omnibus and tram drivers today notified the authorities they would not work tomorrow. The men said they wished to devote the day to celebrating May Day." Banners carried by demonstrators in Panama read: "The bosses are lynching Negroes in the United States!" "Long live the Solidarity of the Latin-American Proletariat with their Brothers of the United States."[20]

In spite of the terror of the Machado regime in Cuba, thousands of unemployed Cubans demonstrated on May Day, 1930. As in 1929, the workers were attacked by police and the Army when, following their parade in Havana, they made their annual pilgrimage to Lenin Square in Regla across the bay where the tree honoring the Russian revolutionary leader was planted. Again two workers died and scores were injured.[21]

The following year (1931), battles between police and May Day demonstrators took place in Havana, Manila, Warsaw, Johannesburg, Barcelona, and Munich. Three were killed in Warsaw and two in

Barcelona.[22] The London *Times* reported that "the honour of the day belonged to an unknown individual who by devious and precipitous ways reached the roof of Berlin University and hoisted the Soviet flag on the central flagstaff." It remained there for several hours before it was torn to pieces by university directors.[23]

May Day meetings were held by the Socialists and then the Communists in Berlin's Lustgarten at the end of Unter der Linden. A battle between the Hitler fascists and the Socialists and Communists followed.[24]

The huge 1931 May Day procession in Madrid, organized by the Socialist Workmen's Associations, was headed by four mounted policemen who cleared a way through the immense crowd. Then followed a row of gaily-dressed children with Phrygian caps behind whom walked the Socialist Ministers and the Mayor of Madrid, who linked arms with members of the Council of the International Federation of Trade Unions, who were meeting in Madrid. Then came the societies with their red banners. When the head of the procession reached the office of the Prime Minister, a delegation entered to present a petition. President Alala Zamora and the Ministers soon appeared on a balcony, and holding the petition in his hand, the president addressed the crowd. He declared that several of the demands, such as the eight-hour day, aid for the unemployed, and compensation for workers injured while at work, were being enacted into law. He hoped that before the next May Day, most of the demands would be granted by the Cortes. Finally, he congratulated the crowd "on an orderliness which was looked on with admiration throughout the world."[25]

Walter Duranty was again awed by the impressive May Day demonstration in Moscow. Commenting on the military parade which alone took three hours, he wrote:[26]

This writer has seen many reviews in peace and war-time, near the front or far from the slightest mutter of reverberating cannon, but he has seen nothing better staged and nothing better representing what it was intended to represent—the strength of the great nation to resist attack. The lesson was not lost on foreign military attachés, more than one of whom admitted their respect and admiration.

The banners carried in the May Day parade in New York on May 1, 1932 demanded the release of Tom Mooney, free rent, unemployment insurance, and old age pensions. In the San Francisco parade the freedom of Tom Mooney was the key demand, and Mrs.

Mary Mooney, mother of Tom Mooney, rode in an open motor car beside her daughter Anna.[27]

Hitler Tries to Steal May Day

In 1933 Adolf Hitler, with the full support and assistance of powerful monopoly capitalists, seized power in Germany. On April 24, Dr. Paul Joseph Goebbels, Nazi Minister of Propaganda and Popular Enlightenment, issued a May Day Manifesto which was carried on the front page of every newspaper in Germany. Addressed "to the whole German people," it announced that May 1st had been made "the festival day of national labor" and called for a celebration in which "Germans of all classes" would "clasp hands" and "in solid formation march into the new future." Class was a thing of the past, "since Marxism is smashed." "Where once the machine guns of the Reds barked, we build a bridge of peace between classes." It was made clear by the Nazis that the day of "national labor" had nothing in common "with international brotherhood in the Marxist sense of the idea."[28]

The Nazis held the May Day rally in the Berlin Lustgarten, the traditional place for the revolutionary working class. In his speech to the workers at Tempelhoferfeld, Hitler predicted that the fascist control would continue in Germany for a thousand years.[29]

The London *Times* praised Hitler and the Nazis for having ended "the glorification of class-warfare and made May Day an occasion for the abolition of class differences and for the unification of workers and employers in the Fascist model."[30] What it did not tell its readers was that despite the Nazi terror, the illegal Communist Party of Germany (KPD) held demonstrations on May 1, 1933, at which the red flag was displayed in Berlin, Chemnitz, Dresden, Halle, Hamburg, Leipzig, Sacssen, Thüringen, and Wittenberg. In Berlin workers raised the cry "Freedom for Thaelman" (the Communist leader who was facing death in a Nazi concentration camp), "The KPD lives," "Not with the murderous Fascism." In Thüringen leaflets distributed to the workers declared: "Let us free Germany from the Terror. Away with the fascist May Day celebration! Long live the revolutionary May Day struggle!" In Weimar leaflets said: "Never with the 1st of May of the Hangman Regime! Long live the May 1st of the revolutionary working class! Who murders the worker cannot honor the working class."[31]

On the very next day after May Day, Hitler signed legislation outlawing the free trade unions in Germany with their membership of 4,000,000, and seized their assets of over 180,000,000 marks. All union leaders who could be seized were taken into custody. Dr. Herbert Ley, president of the Prussian State Council, gave the following reason for the action against the free trade unions: "Marxism today is playing dead, but is not yet altogether abolished. It is therefore necessary to deprive it of its last strength." The *New York Times* noted that the action came one day after "the May Day wooing of German labor."[32]

Unity of Communists and Socialists

In New York City, the United May Day Committee, organized by the Communist Party, called upon the Socialist Party to join the Communists in a "joint May Day rally in Union Square to stop fascism." Although SP leader Norman Thomas opposed the proposal, the Socialists did join with Communists in the May Day parade. Demonstrators chanted, "Right, left, unite, unite for united front." They carried effigies of Hitler as well as banners reading, "Down with Fascism!" "Free the Scottsboro Boys!"* Resolutions adopted at the Union Square meeting of Communists and Socialists read:[33]

> We pledge ourselves to do everything in our power in the shops, unions and organizations to forge the united front of all workers for unemployment and social insurance; immediate adequate cash relief, for increased relief and higher wages to meet the rising cost of living; against Roosevelt's forced wage-cutting inflation program; for a shorter work day without reduction in pay, for the immediate release of Tom Mooney, the Scottsboro boys, the Centralia** and all class prisoners, for Negro rights; against Hitler Fascist terror and pogroms; against the assassin of Italian masses the butcher Mussolini; against imperialist war; smash the provocations against the Soviet Union.

May Day demonstrators in Liege, Belgium, 10,000 strong, marched to the German Consulate, which was flying the Nazi swastika flag. After the police had been overwhelmed, one demonstrator succeeded in

---

*On March 25, 1931, nine Black youths were pulled from a train at Scottsboro, Alabama on which they had been traveling in quest of work, and accused of raping two white girls riding the same freight train. The intervention of the left-wing International Labor Defense (ILD) and worldwide protests finally led to their release.

**On November 11, 1919, IWW headquarters in Centralia, Washington were attacked by members of the American Legion, and in defending themselves, IWW militants killed three Legionnaires. Eight Wobblies were sentenced to from 25 to 40 years in prison.

tearing away a piece of the flag, and a woman demonstrator tore away the rest. The police charged twice, but the demonstrators escaped, carrying the torn flag with them.[34]

May Day, 1933, took place in Austria under the despotic rule of Austrian fascism. Chancellor Engelbert Dollfuss banned the May Day demonstration, and the Ringstrasse was closed from early morning to 11 p.m. by barbed wire entanglements, machine guns, and military guards armed with bayonetted rifles. Persons desiring to use the Ringstrasse had to submit their papers for examination.[35]

On May 2, 1933, the *Weiner Arbeiter-Zeitung*, Socialist organ, cried out: "No May 1 has ever been so celebrated as this one! More than forty years ago, the Vienna workers carried the street, the Ringstrasse, by virtue of their strength and discipline. Since then the State's executive authority has never dared dispute the Street with them on this day. This year it has happened. The Government has forbidden the Vienna workers the street, their Ringstrasse." But the workers had "won the day. From one street they shut us out, and yesterday all Vienna became the marching-route. They forbade us the Ringstrasse demonstration; on eight main streets there were demonstrations of such vast masses that, according to the estimates of all experts, the number of people in a normal May Day demonstration was far surpassed. The route which the 'strollers' of the Vienna working class took yesterday is 40 kilometers long."[36]

The Dollfuss government had also banned the usual torch-light procession of the Socialist youth. The young people defied the ban; they shifted their celebration to the Vienna Woods. "More than 15,000 young people," reported the *Arbeiter-Zeitung*, "marched from all the hilltops of the Vienna Woods to the Dreimarkstein on Sunday, and there in the torch-light made stormy confession to Socialism. Then two gigantic columns marched down into the city filling the streets and the public gardens with defiant battle-songs, chants in chorus and shouts for liberty."[37]

In February, 1934, the First Austrian Republic succumbed to the machine guns, tanks, and howitzers of the brutal Dollfuss regime. On May 1, Dollfuss proclaimed a new constitution which stated that Austria was no longer a Republic, but a corporate state based on the Italian model—the so-called "green" Fascism, with its gallows, prison and concentration camps. The workers' May Day disappeared in Austria.[38]

In its leaflet on May Day 1934, the Communist Party of New York called for unemployment insurance and for unity of action to stop fascism. It also attacked the Socialist leaders of Austria for having "made every concession to Dollfuss, to strengthen fascism and weaken the workers and prepared the way for fascism just as the Socialist leaders did in Germany."[39] That May Day the demonstration in New York was tremendous. Over 20,000 paraded and there were more than 100,000 in Union Square. The reporter for the London *Times* noted: "The Communists and Socialists today had the biggest May Day demonstrations which has ever been seen in New York. The Communists met in Union Square while the Socialists had their meeting in Madison Square Park."[40]

"Hitler seemed to be by far the most popular target—for the derision of both Socialists and Communists, with Mussolini not far behind," went a description of the 1935 May Day demonstrations in New York City. But Carl Brodsky, speaking at the Communist meeting, deplored the Socialists' refusal to agree to a joint parade to strengthen the anti-fascist front as had taken place in 1933. A "surprise speaker" at the meeting was Edwin Markham, the 83-year-old poet, author of the famous poem, "The Man with the Hoe." "Long live the revolutionary tradition of the American working class," Markham told the cheering audience. A "striking feature" of the demonstration was the youth of the demonstrators. "Whole divisions of the parade," wrote a reporter, "seemed to be made up of boys and girls of high school age."[41]

Mass actions and demonstrations continued apace in Canada. The 1932 May Day demonstrators totaled a record-breaking 100,000 participants. In Hamilton, an industrial city just south of Toronto, some 20,000 demonstrators were attacked by police and firemen. After a four-hour battle, eighteen workers were arrested.

In 1935, the Relief Camp Workers Union mobilized for a mass May Day meeting in British Columbia, Canada. The meeting was in part a protest against an earlier police attack on an April gathering of ten thousand unemployed workers and their supporters. On May Day, 15,000 marchers were joined in Stanley Park by 20,000 sympathizers. This was the largest of the actions that continued for some weeks across Canada and resulted in a march to Ottawa, the Canadian capital.[42]

1936: Fiftieth Anniversary

May 1, 1936, was the fiftieth anniversary of the first May Day in 1886. The May Day Manifesto of the Communist Party of the United States began:

May Day is the workers' day, a truly American day for the American working class, baptized in the blood of American workers and carried on through victory and temporary defeat in battle for the workers' demands now and in the future.

Workers were urged to "Down tools on May First" and demonstrate in the streets:

For the six-hour day, for the five-day week without reduction in pay! For higher wages, against the high cost of living....
    For unemployment insurance, old age and social insurance.
    For full social, political and economic equality for the Negro people!...
    For a People's Front against war and fascism! For a Farmer-Labor Party!...

The May Day Manifesto of the Communist International (Comintern) called for the workers to demonstrate "under the international slogans":[43]

For irresistible unity of the working class.
Down with fascist aggressors and war makers.
For bread and freedom.
Down with German fascism—the leading war monger of Europe.
Out of China with the Japanese troops. Long Live a Democratic Japan.
Out of Ethiopia with the Italian invaders.* Long live the Italian people
    from the yoke of fascism!
Down with fascism. Down with capitalism.
Long live Soviet power in all the world, under the flag of Marx-Engels-
    Lenin, forward to the victory of the Socialist World Revolution.
Workers of the World Unite!

In New York, Chicago, San Francisco, Seattle, Detroit and many other cities, the fiftieth anniversary of the birth of May Day was celebrated with parades and demonstrations. In San Francisco the rally was outside of City Hall. Among the slogans carried on signs were: "For A Farmer Labor Party"; "Free All Labor Prisoners"; For A United Front"; "Jobs For Jobless"; "Join the ILD"; and "Free Thaelmann from Nazi Hoodlums" (see photo, p.2).

Communists and Socialists marched together again in New York City on May 1, 1936, along with members of 150 different trade unions

---

*The war against Ethiopia was launched by Benito Mussolini in 1935 and was an outstanding example of imperialism and fascist aggression. Emperor Haile Selassie appealed futilely to the League of Nations for aid.

and more than 150 organizations, all affiliated with the United Labor May Day Committee. A number of the trade unions were associated with the Committee for Industrial Organizations (CIO), founded by a group of AFL unions, headed by UMW President John L. Lewis, to organize the mass production industries on the basis of industrial unionism. Fifty pastors, members of the Ministers' Union of America, made up one contingent. Another was composed of New York's Irish-American transportation workers. One of their special demands was that workers not "be discriminated against when they take off special holidays such as May 1, St. Patrick's Day, etc."[44]

Together with members of the Communist and Socialist parties and other organizations, between 250,000 and 300,000 trade union-ists marched in the 1936 parade, and it was described as "the great-est, largest, most colorful and impressive labor demonstration ever seen in the United States."[45] The *New York Times* limited its de-scription to "one of the largest and most orderly parades in the history of the event."[46]

A gigantic poster, bearing the caption "Shake," was carried by 5,000 Socialist and Communist members of the Fur Workers' Union. "Make New York a 100 percent Union Town," read another Furriers' banner. Other banners carried in the parade included demands for the freedom of Tom Mooney; an end to pogroms in Poland, and the defeat of Hitler and Mussolini. The leading slogan of the Communist Party contingent read: "For a Farmer-Labor Party."

On the reviewing stand in Union Square were the leaders of the Communist and Socialist parties, and officials of a number of CIO and AFL unions. A telegram was read from Tom Mooney and Warren K. Billings urging workers to organize a united front against war and fascism.[47]

On February 26, 1936, a military coup took place in Japan. Tokyo was placed under martial law until the 17th of July, and political open-air gatherings were banned. A nationwide prohibition of the May Day celebration was decreed. Many workers in Japan met at picnics, tea parties, and lectures secretly to celebrate May Day. But in Otaru (Hokkaidi) and Nagoya, workers ignored the prohibition and planned illegal demonstrations. They were quickly arrested. From 1936 to 1945 May Day was not celebrated in Japan.[48]

In Mexico City, 60,000 workers and field laborers paraded on May 1, 1936. Every labor union was represented, and as usual, the dem-onstrators voiced their indignation over "the death of the martyrs in Chicago."[49] In Spain May Day occurred as the fascist forces under Generalissimo Franco threatened the Republic. The stoppage of work was complete in all the larger cities and towns. In Madrid at the head of the great parade were "the unarmed Marxist militia of men and women, mingling with Red Cross units. Collections were made all along the route for funds to buy arms and munitions. . . . Little children, down to the age of four, were led along in bands accompanied by matrons. . . . These little rebels raised their chubby clenched fists with their elders."[50]

Sit-down strikes dominated the headlines in the United States in 1937. Sit downs were effective weapons; workers who were occupying the factories had less fear that their jobs would be taken by scabs, and employers were reluctant to use violence or prolong negotiations for fear of damage to their valuable property. Some sit-down strikes were small while others, such as the General Motors strike in Flint, Michigan, involved 140,000 workers who "sat in" for 44 days—from December 30, 1936, until February 11, 1937. The strike ended in an agreement that recognized the CIO's Auto Workers (UAW) as the collective bargaining agent for its members. The company also agreed not to interfere with the right of its employees to belong to that union.[51]

The following dispatch from San Antonio, Texas appeared in the press on the eve of May Day, 1937: "Two hundred relief and WPA clients started a sit-down strike in City Hall . . . today after their demand for permission to hold a May Day parade was denied."[52]

The United Front Against Fascism

New York's United Front Parade on May 1, 1937 was "the largest and most peaceful of its kind." CIO and AFL unions marched with slogans proclaiming "Unite Against Fascist Aggression," "Crush Anti-Semitism—Weapon of Fascism," "Down with Hitler-Mussolini," "American Labor Wants a Thirty Hour Week," "Admit Nazi Rufugees," "Help Loyalist Spain." In fact, the war waged against Republican Spain by Franco, with the aid of German and Italian fascism, was a major theme of the parade. Another was support for sit-down strikers. "The sit-down strikers from the Jewish Hospital in Brooklyn," wrote a reporter, "convicted under a seldom-invoked law, appeared in the striped uniforms of convicts." One of them carried a banner that read: "Help us out of Jail. End slavery in hospitals."[53]

In Chicago the May Day parade through the loop emphasized aid for Loyalist forces in Spain, organization of the unorganized, a six-hour day, and a five-day week. In New York and Chicago, the May Day meeting featured a letter from Tom Mooney which stated: "I

Section of 1947 New York City May Day parade

hail and commend the American workers for their heroic struggles in the fight to organize and bargain collectively against a brutal exploiting class who are always ready under the guise of law and order to employ their hirelings and assassins and use their puppet public officials to crush the workers."[54]

In France the Popular Front government decreed that May Day "shall henceforth be a national holiday." For the first time in many years May Day was celebrated in Paris and other French cities with processions and open-air meetings, and without a single clash between police or troops and the demonstrators.[55]

Reports from Moscow featured the news that Premier Joseph Stalin had descended from his tribune atop Lenin's tomb in Red Square to greet the Spanish Loyalist delegation marching in the May Day parade. While England, France, the United States and other countries refused to send aid to the Loyalist cause, the Soviet Union was aiding Republican Spain with arms and other supplies.[56]

The Nazi seizure of Austria in the Anschluss of March, 1938, coming on top of fascist intervention in Spain on the side of Franco, was much on the minds of anti-fascist, peace-loving forces as they prepared for May Day. The Communist International's Manifesto for May Day struck heavily at fascist aggression, and called for a common front of the workers of the world. It especially rebuked Great Britain, France, and the United States for failure to check "international fascist brigandage" in Spain, China and Austria, and insisted that "it is a cynical lie to say these countries cannot check such aggression":

> They can check this brigandage but for this it is necessary to accept the proposal of the Soviet Union for joint action against the warmongers by all States that are interested in the preservation of peace. They must reinforce action by measures of economic pressure. Let the fascist bandits be deprived of credit; refuse them the raw materials that are necessary for conducting war; close the channels of trade to them.
>
> Cease blockading Republican Spain, Open the borders and let the Spanish people buy armaments freely. This would be enough to make fascism retreat like a whipped dog.

The Manifesto appealed directly to the Socialist and trade union internationals to take common action with the Communist International in behalf of Loyalist Spain:[57]

> Comrades, get out on the streets May 1. Form a militant column of international united labor front for effective aid for the Spanish people!

Arm the Spanish people!

Proletarians of France—renowned descendants of the Paris Communards—demand immediate removal of the blockade from Republican Spain!

Workers of England, force your ruling classes to end their policy of supporting fascist brigandage and of hostility to the land of socialism!

Proletarians of the United States demand a policy of outlawing the fascist violators of universal peace, of a policy worthy of the tradition of Lincoln and Washington. Demand immediate removal of the embargo on the export of arms to Spain and China.*

In 1938 the Socialists rejected the Communist appeal for continuation of the united front parade. The Communists and Socialists held separate parades and meetings. One hundred veterans of the Abraham Lincoln Battalion, one of the international units mobilized in many countries in support of the Spanish Republic, marched at the head of the Communists and various trade unions, while several wounded and crippled veterans from Spain rode in automobiles. They aroused the greatest applause from the crowds who lined the sidewalks of Eighth Avenue, Thirteenth Street, Fifth Avenue, and Broadway.[58] Although the Central Trades and Labor Council had announced that AFL unions would not participate in the parade, the press reported that "there were a number of AFL unions in line." CIO unions, led by the fur workers and the National Maritime Union were a conspicuous part of the parade. The *New York Times*, in its report of the parade, pointed out that "the Communists and their allies began their marching at 1:30 p.m. at Fifty-sixth Street and Eighth Avenue and were still marching at 8 p.m." On this basis it felt it could agree with the May Day Committee that 200,000 had participated in the parade.[59]

Support for President Franklin D. Roosevelt's recovery and relief programs; passage of a wage-and-hour bill and anti-lynching legislation, freedom for Mooney and Billings, denunciation of fascism, and lifting the embargo on shipments of arms to Loyalist Spain were the leading demands of the demonstrators. The central slogans were: "For Democracy, Jobs, and Peace" and "Unite Against Fascist Aggression."[60]

May 1, 1938, was celebrated in London with processions to Hyde Park "on a very much larger scale than usual." This was attributed to the fact that an appeal had been made by the executives of the

---

*In practice the U.S. Neutrality Act of 1937 operated against the Loyalist government in Spain, which was deprived of aid while the fascists obtained great assistance from Germany and Italy.

Labor Party and the Trades Union Congress to observe this May Day as "Spain Day." The result was a vigorous response and a united front of the Trades Union Congress and "left-wing" elements. The London *Times* reported:

> Spain was certainly very much in the picture. "Arms for Spain are arms for peace" was second only to "Chamberlain must go" as a marching slogan.* There were banners inscribed with the names of members of the Communist Party who had died in Spain, some reading "Stepney workers fallen in Spain—they died that we may live," and others from different parts of London declaring that £5,000 was given by one trade union to help Spain. There were lorries from which appeals were made for medical aid in Spain....On one lorry were stacked some motorbicycles, representing "voluntary industrial aid for Spain." In one procession was a banner declaring: "Irish Republicans greet Spanish Republicans....[61]

The resolution, put simultaneously and carried at all platforms, declared opposition to fascism and war, and a resolve to aid Spain and defend freedom and peace.[62]

The most popular slogan in Paris's May Day parade was "Guns for Spain." In Winnipeg, Canada, 5,000 paraders protested the "action of our government in placing an embargo on war supplies to Loyalist Spain."[63]

No May Day demonstration was allowed in Japan, but in China in territories unoccupied by the Japanese, the workers paraded in protest against the invasion of their country.[64] In Austria, the "Festival of the German People," introduced by the Nazis in 1933 to replace "May Day, with its Marxist connotations," was put into effect for the first time as a symbol of Grossdeutschland (Greater Germany). In Italy the only celebration allowed on May 1 was the Feast of Saint Efislo, at Cagiliari, Sardinia, in memory of the Saint who is said to have saved Cagiliari twice from great danger. In the Scandinavian and Baltic countries of Sweden, Norway, Denmark, Finland, Iceland, May Day demonstrations were numerous, and in Sweden a vigorous effort continued to make May 1 a national holiday. The *New York Times* summed up May Day, 1938, with the comment: "The World Bows to May Day."[65]

In Germany the illegal Communist Party (KPD) distributed leaflets on May Day, 1936 warning the German people that if they did not throw off the yoke of Nazi fascism, they would be plunged by Hitler into another world war. "Never since 1914 is the danger of war

---

*Prime Minister Neville Chamberlain, advocate of appeasement of Hitler.

greater in Europe," the leaflets emphasized. "Hitler is the source of the danger and Thyssen, Krupp and other monopoly capitalists are working with Hitler, and the Gestapo is seeking through murder to still the voices of all anti-war forces."[66]

It took a little over three years of appeasement of Hitler before this warning became a reality. During these years, German fascism, encouraged by European and U.S. imperialism whose aim was to build up Nazi Germany for a war against the Soviet Union, prepared for the second World War. On September 29, 1938, at Munich, the British and French imperialists rejected the call of the Soviet Union for collective security to halt the Nazi seizure of the Sudentenland of Czechoslovakia, and let Hitler have what he wanted. We secured "peace with honor . . . peace in our time" at Munich, British Prime Minister Neville Chamberlain, a leading appeaser of Nazi Germany, told his people.

At Munich, having gained the Sudetenland, Hitler promised to leave the rest of Czechoslovakia alone. But in March 1939 he took over the remainder of the republic. The Soviet Union had been ready to come to Czechoslovakia's aid, but was prevented from doing so. On September 2, 1938, the Soviet Union proposed a joint British-French-Soviet appeal to the League of Nations on aid to Czechoslovakia, joint military talks, and an Anglo-French-Soviet declaration of resolve. England and France at once rejected all three proposals.[67]

In August 1939, its repeated calls for collective security to defeat fascist aggression having been rejected, and determined to prevent, even if temporarily, the plot to direct Hitler's aggression against itself, the Soviet Union signed a non-aggression pact with Germany.

By September 1, Hitler's legions were invading Poland and the Second World War began.

On June 9, 1941, Hitler's armed forces invaded the Soviet Union; just six months later, Imperial Japan attacked Pearl Harbor (December 7, 1941). The United States responded by declaring war on the fascist powers—Germany, Japan and Italy.

Wartime: A Working May Day

During World War II the working class in every country at war with the Axis powers observed May Day by staying on the job and producing the weapons for the destruction of the fascist armies. "A Working May Day" was the description of May 1, 1940, in England and France. "May Day, which should have been a holiday, has been sacrificed to work."[68] The following report from the United States dated May 1, 1942, appeared in the London *Times*:[69]

This is the day when labour traditionally indulges in parades and demonstrations, but this year labour all over the country stayed at work.... Throughout the country workers responded to declarations like that of the New York United May Day Committee, a Communist-dominated organization, which said:

"On this May Day workers of the United States can best demonstrate their unity and determination to destroy Fascism by rededicating themselves with their tools and their skills and energies in factories and shops to the task of ever-increasing and uninterrupted production of the instruments of modern warfare. This May Day assembly lines humming with production are the lines of the march to victory and freedom."

In San Francisco the Communist Party of California distributed 200,000 copies of a manifesto calling on all workers to stay on the job. It urged them to work harder this May Day "to destroy Hitler and the Fascist tyranny."[70]

In Nazi-occupied Europe, May Day rallies were banned. However, according to the Free French Press and Information Service in New York, 50,000 persons demonstrated in the Place Carnot in Lyon in a May Day parade which lasted from 6:30 to 7:30 p.m., sang the *Marseillaise*, and shouted "Long Live de Gaulle" and "String Up Laval."[71]*

In Moscow, the Central Committee of the Soviet Union issued the following slogan for May Day, 1942: "Long live the fighting alliance of the armed forces of the Soviet Union, Great Britain, the United States of America and other freedom-loving peoples waging a just war for liberation against German-Italian imperialism...." The Soviet press featured a May Day call for a second front in Europe. German anti-fascist forces with the Red Army issued May Day leaflets to the German people calling on them to join the workers and peasants of the Soviet Union in the struggle against Nazi fascism, for freedom and socialism.[72]

An outstanding feature of May Day, 1943, were the demonstrations held throughout Nazi-occupied Bulgaria. Demonstrators distributed leaflets which read: "Down with Hitler!" "Kick the Germans out of Bulgaria!" "Long live free Bulgaria!" These slogans were also shouted

---

*Pierre Laval was the puppet ruler of France for the Nazis during the occupation of the country.

by crowds in front of the Parliament buildings in Sofia. The demonstrations were organized by the Bulgarian "Liberty Front" and the anti-fascist Troka organization.[73]

A May Day address to the underground labor movement in Europe was delivered by shortwave on May 1, 1943 by the united AFL-CIO-Railroad Brotherhoods in the United States. It promised the workers in the Axis-controlled countries that "American workers will continue outproducing the enemy in tanks, planes, and ships."[74]

The London *Times* featured the statement in Stalin's Order of the Day for May 1, 1943, that declared: "The blow at the enemy from the East dealt by the Red Army merged with the blow from the West dealt by the troops of our allies into one joint blow." "The 'substantial' contribution of the United States and Great Britain to the Russian achievement," the *Times* observed with great satisfaction, "is acknowledged in an ungrudging spirit."[75]

Fifty thousand workers celebrated May Day in New York on May 2, 1943, in a "Labor for Victory Rally" at Yankee Stadium. Sponsored by the Labor for Victory and Unity Committee, the rally was endorsed by the New York Industrial Council of the CIO. But the then right-wing State CIO Council, the AFL Central Trades and Labor Council of Greater New York, the International Ladies' Garment Workers' Union, and the Amalgamated Clothing Workers refused to do so on the ground that it was a "Communist-dominated gathering." Despite attacks from conservative forces, New York's Mayor Fiorello H. LaGuardia and Senator Claude Pepper of Florida addressed the conference. Answering the charge that the rally was "a Communist maneuver," LaGuardia pointed to two planes flying overhead, and said: "Uncle Sam didn't ask those boys to what party they belong."[76]

Speaking on radio from Moscow on April 29, 1944, Wilhelm Pieck sent May Day greetings to the German people. "This month of May must and will be the last under Hitler's regime and Hitler's war," he predicted. "Then will our people enjoy a free Germany in peace with other peoples and in friendship with all. Long live the militant May Day. Long live the free, democratic Germany."[77]

On May 1, 1944, members of the illegal Communist Party of Germany in the Buchenwald concentration camp a few miles from Weimar, met secretly with Russian, Czech, Dutch, French, Belgian, and Polish Communists to celebrate May Day. They sang a workers' song and listened to several speakers. Robert Siewert, a German communist, spoke on the meaning of May Day, the role of the Soviet Army in the struggle against fascism, and paid tribute to the memory of Ernst Thaelmann, murdered by the Nazis. "No retreat before Fas-

cism," he declared. "Hold high the banner of proletarian internationalism . . ." The demonstrators then issued a handwritten leaflet
calling for freedom from fascism and the end of the war.[78]

Victorious May Day

"On this the twenty-seventh celebration of May Day officially observed in the Soviet Union, the Russians will have many reasons to
celebrate," observed the *New York Times*. "Leningrad, Novgorod,
Smolensk, Kiev, Odessa and most of the Crimea, the Ukraine and
White Russia have been torn back from the Germans, and the Red
Army is fighting in Romania and at the entrance of Czechoslovakia."[79]
The Soviet Union celebrated the third May Day of the Patriotic War
without the traditional Red Square demonstration, but with brilliant
holiday festivities, cheered by Premier Stalin's May Day proclamation that Germany had lost the war.[80]

On September 8, 1943, after Mussolini had been deposed and a
new government set up under Marshal Pietro Badoglio, the Italian
government signed an unconditional surrender. Although Italy was
still occupied by strong German forces, which Hitler had in fact
strengthened, the Badoglio government restored May 1 as an official
labor holiday. "It may be recalled," noted the *New York Times*, "that
one of the Fascist regime's first edicts was the closing down all
demonstrations on this day."[81]

Actually, the *Times* was not pleased by this action in liberated
Italy, and in an editorial on May 3, 1944, it expressed the hope that
after the victory over fascism in Europe, May Day would be replaced
by the first Monday in September as Labor Day. "Let us hope that
it will become such in reconstructed Europe, and be there, as it is
here, no festival of a class but a general holiday."[82]

The *Times* was to be disappointed. Fascism, which had brought
such indescribable misery upon so many millions of people, was
defeated in the spring of 1945. In the first weeks of April, the Russian
troops fought their way into Vienna. After eleven years of fascism,
for the first time May 1 was again celebrated in liberty. Socialists
and Communists together, as together they had fought in the resistance against fascism, conducted impressive demonstrations on
May Day. In its May Day 1945 proclamation, the Socialist Party of
Austria said:[83]

> We greet our Socialist fighters who today are still languishing in the
> convict prisons and concentration camps of the Swastika-fascists, and

shall never forget the heroes who had to lose their lives in the fight for freedom. Today our thoughts and burning wishes are with them all. And so we celebrate this 1 May, filled with proud consciousness that the magnitude and sublimity of the goals we fight for inspires us, and with the feeling of profoundest solidarity and union with the Proletarians of all lands and peoples.

May Day, 1945, found Berlin in its "last throes," with Red Army troops storming the blazing administration heart of the city, having captured the German Reichstag and run up the Russian victory flag over the Nazi monument. In a May Day order of the day, Premier Stalin said the war was approaching its end and declared: "The last assault is on!" After almost four years, the blackout ended in Moscow on May Day, and the "honored units of the victorious Red Army" were reviewed by Stalin "on the greatest and happiest May 1 celebration that has taken place in the Soviet Union since the initial holiday in 1918, when this fledgling Socialist state was proud to have exceeded the span of life of the Paris Commune."[84]

Poster by Arno Mohr for the German Socialist Unity
Party, May Day, 1946

Cover, Souvenir Program for May Day
demonstration, London, 1946

May Day, 1950, Berlin. A farmworker signs the Stockholm Appeal
to ban atomic weapons.

7

The Cold War Affliction
(1946–1959)

It was the first of May, 1946, the first May Day since the triumph of the socialist and democratic forces over fascism. Against the background of shattered buildings, about 300,000 German workers took part in the May Day demonstration organized by the Socialist Unity Party (SED), an amalgam of the Social Democrats and the Communists. Carrying red banners, they marched into the Lustgarten in the Russian section of Berlin.[1] "The working class marches," declared the May Day Manifesto of the SED, "after so many shameful years, in brotherly struggle under the banner of unity. For the first time since May 1, 1933, May 1st will be ours. We will never forget the sacrifice of the Soviet people which made possible the liberation of Germany."[2]

In Thüringen, the SED Manifesto declared: "May 1, 1946, will for all times remain a historic day, a proud day of triumph of the unified working class, a day of the strength of the democratic anti-fascist forces, a day of victory."[3] Socialists and Communists marched in separate demonstrations in Vienna, but the size and enthusiasm was "on the old scale for the first time in thirty years."[4]

The headline in the New York *Amsterdam News*, read, "50,000 marchers out to celebrate May Day." The Black weekly pointed out that it was the first May Day parade in New York City since 1941. The United May Day Committee put the figure at 60,000 and said 250,000 watched the parade. Five hundred Army and Navy veterans of World War II, including fifty officers, marched in the Communist Party contingent. They marched in their uniforms even though the Army and the Navy said it was illegal to do so. Six officers of AFL unions joined in sponsoring the May Day parade despite their being advised by the Central Trades and Labor Council that the demonstration had been repudiated by the Council, and that no AFL banners or insignia were to be displayed.* In addition, a rank and file contingent of nearly 2,000 dressmakers and cloakmakers joined other AFL groups in the parade.[5]

The National Maritime Union, with the largest contingent of marchers, "had the honor of leading the parade." The seamen carried banners reading: "Break with Franco Spain"; "Grant Puerto Rico Independence"; "Rankin and Bilbo Must Go";** "Seamen Want Decent Working Conditions."[6] Among the other CIO unions in the parade were the Furriers Joint Council and Joint Board; Local 65 of the Wholesale and Warehouse Workers' Union; the United Office and Professional Workers of America; United Electrical, Radio and Machine Workers; United Furniture Workers, and United Shoe Workers.[7]

The official theme of the demonstration was "World Labor Unity, Peace and Progress." The official slogans were "End Diplomatic Relations with Franco Spain"; "Withdrawal of British Troops from Greece"; "Liberation of India"; "Abolition of the Rankin Committee to Investigate Un-American Activities"; "Preserve the Office of Price Administration." The uniformed veterans also carried banners with the slogans: "Veterans March for Peace"; "Defeat Efforts of Reactionaries to Provoke War with the Soviet Union."[8]

In Moscow, the chief slogans of May Day, 1946 were "Working people of all lands Fight to destroy fascism!"; "Expose reactionaries and fascist hangers-on who are sowing enmity among the peoples"; "Let us be vigilant in protecting the peace that has been won."[9]

May Day in Japan awakened from its dormancy, as half a million paraded in Tokyo—the first May Day celebration since 1934. Their banners demanded a seven-hour day and removal of the Shidehara Cabinet;† above all, they demanded food. Because of postwar inflation and wartime devastation, their lives were on the brink of ruin, and not even the presence of white-helmeted U.S. military police could keep them from singing "Red Flag" to the tune of "Maryland, My Maryland" and the "May Day" song to the tune of an ancient Japanese children's ditty. The words of the latter went:

---

*These notices went to the Bakery and Confectionary Workers, Local 1; Jewelry Workers, Local 1; Hotel and Club Employees, Local 6; Cooks and Chefs, Local 87; Painters Local 965, and Printing Pressmen, Local 447. (*New York Times*, May 1,2, 1946.)

**Rankin and Bilbo were two of the most viciously racist U.S. Senators, both from Mississippi.

†At the time of Japan's surrender, Baron Shidehara was appointed Prime Minister.

Listen, hear the sound of
marching feet. The world's
workers are parading and
demonstrating on May Day.

Kyuchi Tobuda, secretary general of the Communist Party and
Kuaju Kato, member of the executive committee, read the official
slogans: "Production sabotage and inflation are caused by the capitalists who drink our blood!"; "Food for workers!"; "A Minimum Wage
Regulated by Living Cost!"[10]

Korea celebrated its first May Day since liberation from Japan.
Parades were prohibited, but a meeting was held in Seoul's athletic
field, and was addressed by Park Heun Yung, secretary general of
the Communist Party. In their May Day issue, left-wing newspapers
called for the establishment of a "democratic people's government
in Korea in which no class distinctions would be recognized."[11]

May Day was celebrated in India at a big meeting organized by
the All-India Trade Union Council. It was addressed by Communist
Rajani Palme Dutt, who came from England to bring a message of
international solidarity and support for the coming struggle for national freedom.[12] From Caracas, Venezuela came the following dispatch: "This city was subjected today to the equivalent of a one-
day general strike as practically all workers laid down their tools
in celebration of May Day and effectively tied up all normal activity."[13]

Truman Launches the Cold War

On April 12, 1945, Franklin D. Roosevelt died. Soon after the end
of World War II, his successor, Harry S Truman, launched the Cold
War, joining with long-time anti-Soviet forces in a policy of confrontation against the former wartime ally who, at a terrible cost in
lives, had played the major role in the destruction of fascism. In
March, 1947, he initiated the "Truman Doctrine," asking Congress
for $400 million—supposedly to save Greece and Turkey "from Com-
munist conquest." At the same time, Truman ordered a full-scale
"loyalty investigation" of all present and prospective federal employees. In compliance with the President's order, Attorney General
Tom Clark issued in December, 1947, a list of ninety organizations
deemed disloyal to the United States. One of the organizations so
listed was the New York United May Day Committee.[14]

Efforts to counteract May Day as a day of international labor
solidarity were made in the United States as far back as the 1920s.

In fact, in 1920, the National Security League, a jingoistic, anti-labor, pro-business organization launched a campaign to have the mayors of 200 cities sponsor patriotic days on May 1 to offset the May Day demonstrations.[15] This campaign won the support of the American Federation of Labor. In 1923 Samuel Gompers told a *New York Times* reporter that a patriotic celebration on May 1 should be supported by workers in the United States, for May Day had "none of the European meaning" to American workers. "May Day means nothing more to American labor than it does to any other American."[16]

The AFL leaders also joined the campaign to promote the idea of celebrating May Day as Child Health Day. In response, Congress passed a resolution in 1928 directing the President to issue a proclamation calling upon the people of the United States to observe May 1 as Child Health Day. In its report to the 1928 AFL convention, the Executive Council hailed this action:

> The Communists still maintain May 1 as Labor Day. Hereafter, May 1 will be known as Child Health Day.... The object is to create sentiment for year-round protection of the health of children. It is a most worthy purpose. At the same time May 1 will no longer be known as either strike day or Communist Day.[17]

Unity of the Left—Center Coalition Broken

None of these efforts to distract attention from May Day as a workers' holiday had very much effect, as the size and enthusiasm of the demonstrations during the 1930s testify. But with the advent of the Cold War, the United States was plunged into the anti-Communist hysteria of McCarthyism with its persecution and jailings under the Smith Act and the McCarren Act.* To break the growing labor militancy and strike wave that arose in the aftermath of World War II, Congress passed the Taft-Hartley law.** Within the CIO, Wal-

---

*The Smith Act, passed in 1940, made it illegal for a person to advocate "overthrowing...any government in the United States by force," or to "affiliate" with groups teaching the doctrine. The law was clearly directed against thought and not against action. The McCarran-Wood Act, also known as the Internal Security Act, passed in September, 1950, required registration with the Attorney-General of Communist organizations, their affiliates, and their officers. Data relating to finances and publications also had to be filed.

**The Taft-Hartley Act, passed in 1947, increased the power of employers and limited the power of trade unions. Among other things, it permitted the hiring of non-union workers, required a cooling-off period before permitting strikes, and forced union officials to swear that they did not belong to the Communist Party.

ter Reuther, James B. Carey, Emil Rieves, and later Philip Murray broke the former Left-Center Coalition which had been in existence since the formation of the industrial union campaign. In its stead, they embarked on a policy of expulsion of the Left and progressive leadership and union-raiding.

At the eleventh CIO convention in 1949, a resolution was introduced to expel the 50,000-member United Electrical, Radio, and Machine Workers of America. Without a trial or hearing, the resolution to expel was passed. The charter of the electrical workers was handed to James B. Carey, the leading CIO Cold War advocate. The next day, the Union of Farm Equipment and Metal Workers was expelled and the union's jurisdiction turned over to the United Auto Workers. Expulsion of the Fur and Leather Workers Union; the United Office and Professional Workers; the International Mine, Mill, and Smelter Workers; the International Longshoremen and Warehousemen's Union; the Food, Tobacco, Agricultural and Allied Workers Union; the United Public Workers; the American Communications Association; the National Union of Marine Cooks and Stewards; and the International Fishermen and Allied Workers followed. In all, eleven progressive unions, with almost 1 million members, were expelled from the CIO as "Communist-dominated."

While this dismal procedure was under way, James B. Carey told the leaders of an American Legion-sponsored "anti-Communist" conference in New York: "In the last war we joined the Communists to fight the fascists; in another war we will join the fascists to fight the Communists."[18]

On the eve of May Day, 1948, the *New York Times* referred to the forthcoming "traditional May Day parade of the Communist Party." This was sharply criticized by Sam Wiseman, executive director of the May Day Committee, who pointed out that the committee "is composed of sixty trade union, fraternal, civic and tenant-consumer organizations representing 250,000 people. The Communist Party is one of the organizations that will march supporting the slogans, 'Peace,' 'Repeal of the Taft-Hartley Law,' 'Higher Wages and Lower Prices,' 'Preserve the Bill of Rights,' and 'Make Jim Crow illegal.' "[19] His reply had no effect; the press not only in the United States but in a number of other capitalist countries reflected the Cold War atmosphere and continued to link May Day solely to the Communist Party.[20]

There were two parades in New York City on May 1, 1948. The first was the traditional parade, and the other was the Loyalty Day parade of the Veterans of Foreign Wars. New York City officially proclaimed May 1 as Loyalty Day, and the *New York Times* suggested that the "observance of May 1 as Loyalty Day should be a national holiday."[21] In the succeeding years, New York State and several cities followed the practice, and in 1955, President Dwight Eisenhower proclaimed May 1 to be Loyalty Day. About the same time May 1st was declared Law Day.[22]

On May Day, 1948, AFL Vice-President Matthew Woll, the leading anti-Communist in the Federation, made an appeal over shortwave radio, with the assistance of the U.S. State Department, to workers of Europe. His message, broadcast in twenty languages, assured the workers that the AFL was ready to help them if they rose up against the Soviet Union and/or the Communist Party of their respective countries.[23] It became a regular practice for AFL and CIO leaders to address workers in the Federal Republic of Germany or speak over "Radio Free Europe" on May Day with anti-Communist messages. A frequent speaker was Irving Brown, the European representative of the AFL and leader of efforts to disrupt the European labor movement and to gain support among European workers for the anti-Soviet North American Atlantic Treaty Organization (NATO). Others were George Meany, president of the AFL and later of the AFL-CIO, Walter Reuther and Victor Reuther of the United Auto Workers, (CIO) and Philip Murray of the United Steel Workers, who became CIO president after the resignation of John L. Lewis in 1944.[24]

Led by the Communist Party, the Tokyo May Day demonstration in 1948 sent a petition to General Douglas MacArthur, U.S. administrator in Japan, pointing out that labor had worked to build a peaceful, democratic Japan, but "the capitalist classes and public prosecutors who act in collaboration with the capitalists are adopting oppressive measures against the workers encroaching upon their freedom and livelihood." The resolutions adopted by the meeting warned of "the rebirth of imperialistic fascist power in our country."

In Bangkok, Siam (soon to be renamed Thailand), May Day was celebrated for the first time on May 1, 1948, at a rally attended by 50,000. The event marked the inauguration of the Siamese Labor Union.[25]

On February 9, 1950, Senator Joseph V. McCarthy of Wisconsin, speaking in West Virginia, charged that the United States had been shorn of its strength by "traitors" working in the interests of the Soviet Union. Thus began a new era of witch-hunts in which thousands of Americans were confronted with wild charges of disloyalty. Many lost their jobs and others were sent to prison. The victory of the Chinese Communists in 1949 and the establishment of the People's Republic of China, was seen by McCarthy and other anti-Communists as due to "pro-Communists" in the U.S. State Department.

On June 26, 1950, charging that North Korea had invaded South Korea, President Truman ordered U.S. naval and air units to support South Korea in what was actually a civil war. On the following day, June 27, with the Soviet delegate absent, the United Nations Security Council urged UN members to join in the attack against North Korea. U.S. troops comprised about four-fifths of the UN forces in Korea. By the time the war ended in 1953, over 54,000 U.S. soldiers had been killed and many more thousands wounded. The national hysteria against Communists and progressives, stirred up by the government and abetted by the media, reached new heights during the Korean War.

An indication of the effort to use May Day to stir up anti-Communist hysteria during this period occurred on the eve of May 1, 1950. The Mayor of Moswee, Wisconsin, 180 miles north of Milwaukee, announced that the mill town would be taken over on May Day by "mock Communists in a May Day Americanism demonstration sponsored by the Wisconsin American Legion." Benjamin Gitlow, former Communist who was now a paid informer for Senator McCarthy and the House Un-American Activities Committee, was in charge of technical operations for the Legion in Moswee.

Communists from Milwaukee distributed leaflets in Moswee that declared:

So this is supposed to be Communism—says who?
    The boss—the guy who owns the mills.
    American Legion big shots—who do what the mill owners
    tell them to . . .
    Stool pigeons—who are paid plenty by the mills for lying and
    double-crossing labor unions and other organizations.

Not to be outdone by the American Legion, the Veterans of Foreign Wars staged a Loyalty Day parade in Chicago as a "protest against Communism and its May Day demonstrations."[26]

In this atmosphere it became increasingly difficult to uphold the May Day tradition in the United States. Still, the effort was made. On the eve of May Day, 1951, the May Day Committee of the Furriers Joint Council and the Joint Board of Fur Dressers and Dyers' Union (New York) called on union members to march in the May Day parade "in defense of your working conditions and standard of living," and "above all . . . to save the peace of the world from the advocates of the Cold War." It made it clear that "consistent with their long-standing anti-fascist policy, the fur workers will reject the administration's incendiary program of renazifying and rearming Germany as a giant step to World War III." The May Day Committee called for "an end to the senseless bloodletting in Korea," and demanded that "all the parties concerned sit down and peaceably negotiate a settlement."

On May 1, 1951, the fur workers joined with other left-wing unions, a number of which, like the furriers, had been expelled from the CIO as "communist-dominated," and the Communist Party in the May Day parade. The *New York Times* called it "the shortest parade in years." The marchers chanted:[27]

> One, two, three, four
> We don't want another war.
> Five, six, seven, eight,
> We don't want a Fascist state.

Pelted with "salvos of eggs" by hoodlums, the marchers continued to parade, carrying banners with slogans: "Save Willie McGee!" "Justice for the Trenton Six!" "Vindication for the Martinsville Seven!" "Freedom for the Twelve!" The first three slogans referred to Black prisoners facing execution or long terms in prison as a result of frameups. The fourth referred to the Communist leaders found guilty in a biased trial of violating the Smith Act.[28]*

Marches Banned, Rallies Persist

In 1949, the government banned political marches in London, and the London Trades' Council's May Day demonstration was abandoned. When the Communists attempted to march, they were attacked by police. The London Trades' Council substituted a mass meeting in Trafalgar Square at which resolutions were adopted condemning the ban on the traditional right to march on May Day.[29]

In New York City the ban on the traditional May Day parade came in 1953 when Police Commissioner George P. Monaghan declared that "the anti-Communist feelings of other citizens would create a potential riot-laden situation." In reply, Leon Straus, chairman of

---

*The Communist leaders were found guilty in federal court in New York of "conspiracy to teach and advocate the duty and necessity to overthrow the U.S. Government by force and violence . . . ." and not for engaging in any acts. In June, 1951, the United States Supreme Court voted 6–2 to uphold the conviction. Speaking for the majority, Chief Justice Vinson said: "Certain kinds of speech are so undesirable as to warrant criminal prosecution."

the United Labor and People's May Day Committee, declared that Monaghan had "contempt for his own police department when he says it can't preserve law and order." Monaghan thereupon replied that the real reason for the ban was that the May Day Committee had been listed by the Attorney General as "subversive," that the Federal Subversive Activities Control Board had ruled that the sponsors of the May Day parade were "puppets of a foreign power, and while American boys are dying in Korea in mortal conflict with the puppets of the same foreign power, I believe that it would be an insult to the people of this city . . . to permit these same puppets to march in our streets with the sanction of the municipal government."⁰ It was in this period that the crime was committed of sentencing Ethel and Julius Rosenberg to death and Morton Sobell to thirty years' imprisonment, allegedly for having given the Soviet Union the secrets of the atomic bomb, for which no real evidence was actually presented during the trial. In handing down the sentence of death, Judge Irving Kaufman declared that the Rosenbergs' supposed action was "worse than murder," since it was responsible for thousands of deaths of U.S. soldiers in Korea. Despite worldwide protests, the Rosenbergs were executed on June 19, 1953.[31]

The Committee appealed the ban to the State Supreme Court, but Judge Carroll Walter upheld it, stating that a parade down Eighth Avenue would interfere with traffic. The Committee proposed alternative routes, but Commissioner Monaghan rejected the offer, stating that he objected to the "purposes of the parade sponsors." However, the May Day Committee was still permitted to use Union Square for its rally, which Leon Straus called a "partial victory."[32]

Norman Thomas called the ban on the May Day parade "an invitation to future mob violence."[33] But the *New York Times* argued that the "important thing" in the Commissioner's order, and its "saving grace, is that it recognizes and protects the right to assemble." However, a reader of the *Times* charged the paper with having capitulated to "our present 'public opinion' engendered by McCarthyism. This new spirit is one of fear."[34] Mayor Impelliteri answered criticism of the ban by stating bluntly: "The Communists do not belong in the streets of New York." He made it clear that had there been a parade, the police would have used force to break it up.[35]

The May Day Committee claimed that 25,000 had appeared at the Union Square rally while the *New York Times* put the figure at 5,000. The demonstrators carried banners with the slogans: "End the War in Korea!" "Welcome Home All the Boys!" "Protest the ban on the

67-year-old right to parade!" "Freedom to the Rosenbergs!" "Resistance to McCarthyism!" "End Police Brutality Against Negroes
and Puerto Ricans!" In the leading speech at the meeting, the Black
artist and freedom fighter Paul Robeson said: "We are part of the
hundreds of millions who have, for the first time in history, the
strength to impose peace. We dedicate ourselves here on this May
Day that peace shall prevail." Greetings were read from the central
organization of Chinese Trade Unions and the All-India Trade Union
Congress.[36]

The United May Day Committee was denied a parade permit again
in 1954, and this time, the meeting in Union Square was restricted
to only one and one-half hours—from 6:30 to 8:00 p.m. However,
the Businessmen's Association of Fourteenth Street was permitted
to use the Square for eight hours for a loyalty meeting. The May
Day Committee protested to Mayor Robert F. Wagner that it was
"totally unfair" to give "an employers' group eight hours and labor
one and a half hours on labor's great holiday." Its request for at
least three hours was denied, but the time was extended to two
hours.[37]

The crowd in Union Square was estimated at 15,000 by the May
Day Committee. The meeting called for an end to war in Indochina,
a $1.25 minimum wage, equal rights for Negroes, defeat of Mc-
Carthyism, for an effective Fair Employment Practices Commission
(FEPC), and independence for Puerto Rico. In his speech, Paul Robeson predicted that "People's China will be seated at the United
Nations." Helen Sobell, wife of Morton Sobell (who was sentenced
to thirty years in prison in the Rosenberg case) said that her husband
"will not buy his freedom by bearing false witness, for he cannot be
dishonorable; he cannot reject the truth."[38]

The following year, New York City denied permission to parade
or to hold a Union Square meeting on May Day or on April 30. The
City claimed that prior permits had been granted for patriotic programs to the Fourteenth Street businessmen. As a result, the Progressive Workers and People's Committee for May Day was compelled
to call the May Day meeting in Union Square for April 29. The theme
was "Peace, Jobs and Democracy," and banners read: "Support the
30-Hour Week," "East-West Trade Means Jobs," "Not a Single American Boy to Defend Quemoy,"* "Big Five Talks for World Peace,"
"Stop School Jim Crow," "Enact FEPC."

Once again Paul Robeson spoke, and this time he hailed the Ban-

*An island off mainland China occupied by the forces of Chiang Kai-shek.

dung Conference of Third World Nations. "The lesson of Bandung," he said, "is that peoples of diverse cultures and systems can meet, discuss and reach agreements on how to promote the peace of the world." Another speaker was Alexander Trachtenberg, the 70-year-old head of International Publishers and long-time Marxist educator, who had been imprisoned under the Smith Act but had been released two years before his sentence expired. "I underestimated by two years the anti-McCarthy sentiment in the country," he explained.[39]

For the third successive year, the 1956 May Day Committee was prohibited from holding its May Day rally in Union Square on May 1. Once again the New York City Park Department gave the Fourteenth Street Association permission to hold a patriotic rally in the Square on May Day. The Trade Union Committee for May Day was permitted to hold its meeting on April 30 from 3:00 to 5:00 p.m.[40] Between 3,000 and 4,000 demonstrators were at Union Square carrying signs: "30-hour week; $1.25 minimum wage"; "Repeal Witch-Hunt Laws"; "Atomic Energy for Peace, Not War"; "Let Robeson Sing to the World. Grant His Passport"; Outlaw Anti-Semitism and Jim Crow." Benjamin Davis, Jr., Black Communist leader and former New York City Councilman, made his first outdoor speech since being released from a Smith Act prison sentence. Morris Cimmerman, who had witnessed the first May Day celebration in 1886, also spoke. He linked the two May Day celebrations—the historic demand at the first May Day for the eight-hour day and the call for the thirty-hour week in 1956.[41]

The 1957 May Day celebration in New York was sponsored by the Committee for Socialist Unity, headed by Clifford T. McAvoy, American Labor Party candidate for Mayor. The Committee called a rally at Central Plaza Hall, Second Avenue and Seventh Street, on May 1. (Union Square had been given by the Park Department for May Day to the Fourteenth Street Business Men's Association.) The speakers included Dr. W. E. B. DuBois, distinguished Black historian and peace advocate; Rev. A. J. Muste, the veteran pacifist; Conrad Lynn, Black civil rights attorney, and George Blake Charney for the Communist Party.

Banners decorating the hall read: "End segregation—Enforce the Constitution"; "Restore the Bill of Rights"; "Ban Nuclear Weapons —Stop the Tests Now"; "Support the Pilgrimmage of Prayer." The last slogan was a reference to the rally for civil rights planned for May 17 in Washington, D.C.[42]

"Commercial newspapers are congratulating themselves prematurely with the claim that great May Day demonstrations are ended because there was no Union Square gathering," declared the *Daily Worker* on May 3, 1957. "From the spirit of the Central Plaza meeting...comes the promise of greater May Days to come." It credited the Left with having "maintained the tradition of May Day." But it added: "Now it must again find the way to encourage and help unite the great mass of organized labor to develop all-inclusive May Day celebrations of tomorrow."[43]

Kept out of Union Square again in 1958, the left-wing May Day rally occurred on the evening of May 1 in Carnegie Hall. This time the sponsor was *The Worker*, Communist weekly. Vicente Lombardo Toledano, the Mexican labor leader, was scheduled as the main speaker, but he was unable to obtain a visa because of his left-wing views.[44]

Union Square on May 1, 1959 was again taken over by the Fourteenth Street Businessmen's Association, which hailed its success since 1954, when the Association and the N.Y. City government decided "to rid the park of the Communist taint of former years." The Veterans of Foreign Wars called it "a companion move to the Loyalty Day parade on May 1st," and praised Mayor Wagner for proclaiming May Day as "Union Square U.S.A. Day."[45]

The left-wing organizations celebrated May Day in Union Square on May 2, sponsored by the Trade Union Committee 1959 May Day Celebration, with Louis Weinstock, a veteran Communist militant in the Painters' Union, as chairman. "Three thousand Turn Out for a Folksy May Day Party," wrote Guy Talese in his report in the *New York Times*. He described the meeting as "orderly as a church social," adding that "nobody advocated the overthrow of anything."[46]

May Day Thrives Around the World

In London, the traditional May Day parade to Hyde Park reappeared on May 1, 1955, although it took place in a downpour. "With clothes soaked by continuous rain," said the report in the London *Times*, "a huge procession of marchers arrived at Hyde Park yesterday in London's May Day demonstration."[47] Nothing worthy of much comment in the commercial press relating to May Day appeared, however, until 1958 when a number of people, including four members of St. Pancreas Borough Council in London, were taken away in a police van from a May Day rally organized by the St. Pancreas and Holborn Trades Council. The arrests were caused by the fact that shortly after 7:00 a.m. the Red Flag had been hoisted over the town hall in celebration.[48]

May Day demonstrations in the German Democratic Republic, beginning in 1949, were featured by huge parades through Marx-Engels Platz to Unter der Linden. On May 1, 1955 the demonstrators carried portraits of Schiller, Beethoven, Bach, and Gerhart Hauptmann along with those of national and world Communist leaders.[49] At the 1956 parade, the national people's army marched for the first time in public at the head of the May Day demonstration.[50]

On May 1, 1958, demonstrations were held in many cities of the Federal Republic of Germany against plans of the government to equip the West German military forces with nuclear weapons. Trade unions in Dusseldorf, Munich, Frankfurt, Hamburg, West Berlin, and smaller cities led the demonstrators. "The parades marking the labor holiday," wrote a reporter, "were largely given over to a campaign against the atom death being sponsored by the government of Chancellor Adenauer. Bonn has agreed to arm its forces with tactical atomic weapons on the recommendation of the North Atlantic Treaty Organization (NATO)." Over three million people in the Federal Republic demonstrated against nuclear armaments. Slogans all over Germany consisted of innumerable variations of the theme: "No Nuclear Weapons!"[51]

The racist government of South Africa took special precautions on the eve of May Day, 1950, to curb "Freedom" rallies on the first of May called by the Communist Party. The aim was to "transform May Day into 'Freedom Day' to demonstrate against the policies of the nationalist government."[52] At the same time, the Youth League of the African National Congress, headed by Nelson Mandela, issued a call for a "national stoppage of work for one day as a mark of protest against the reactionary policy of the Government." May 1, 1950 was chosen for the demonstration of protest. All public gatherings, except of a religious or sporting character, were banned from April 30 to May 3. "To enforce this ban," wrote a reporter from Capetown, "it concentrated police reserves and army units in industrial areas of the Transvaal." When demonstrators insisted on holding "Freedom" rallies on May Day, the police in Johannesburg fired on the demonstrators, killing nineteen Blacks and injuring thirty-eight.[53]

For the first time in its history, Poland celebrated May Day on May 1, 1950, as an official holiday, and close to a million Poles marched in Warsaw.

On the eve of May Day in 1951, the government headed by Prime Minister Mohammed Mossadegh in Iran nationalized the nation's oil resources, expropriating all the assets of the Anglo-Iranian Oil Company. "As his first act of power," wrote a reporter from Tehran, "Dr. Mossadegh removed the chief of staff and the Chief of Police last night and made them rescind a previous order banning the May Day demonstration."[54] On May Day, Iran's outlawed Tudeh (Communist) Party packed Parliament Square in Tehran with 30,000 demonstrators. They hailed the "heroic nations of the Soviet Union," and cheered references to "Liberated China, the Hope of the world," and "Valiant Korea in her struggle against the American aggressors."[55]

May Day slogans in the Soviet Union in the 1950s emphasized the need for collective security for all peace-loving people, and a stronger struggle against the rebirth of German militarism. In 1954 it was noted that "Soviet-Chinese collaboration is a powerful factor for preserving peace and assuring the security of the peoples of all countries."[56] Among the 69 slogans issued for May Day, 1955 by the Central Committee of the Communist Party of the Soviet Union was one wishing the people of the Soviet Union, Great Britain and the United States success in their "struggle for lessening international tension, for peaceful co-existence of the states and guaranteeing a stable peace in the whole world."[57]

In December, 1959 the Soviet Union accepted a proposal by the United States for a Spring Summit Conference. But Premier Khrushchev pointed out in a letter to President Dwight Eisenhower that the proposed date of April 26 was inconvenient because it conflicted with the big Soviet May Day holiday. He suggested May 4 as the day for the summit.[58]

Hundreds of thousands of Chinese paraded in Peking and other cities on May Day after the formation of the People's Republic of China. In 1953, the fourth May Day celebration since liberation in 1949, the paraders carried the cumbersome slogan: "Support the statements issued by China, Korea, and the Soviet Union in the Korean armistice negotiations and strive to achieve an armistice in Korea and a peaceful settlement of the Korean question." Among the other 55 slogans were: "Oppose American imperialistic occupation of Taiwan;* Oppose American blockade of China"; "Oppose American imperialists using Japan as a military base;" and "Strengthen trade with other People's Democracies."[59]

One of the 65 slogans for May Day, 1954, called for a ban on atomic and hydrogen bombs, and in 1955 one called for the liberation of Taiwan. Another called upon all peoples to "work for peaceful co-existence among countries with different social systems to

*Defeated by the Chinese Communists, Chang Kai-shek withdrew to Taiwan.

solve international disputes by peaceful negotiations." Still others asked for peaceful solutions to the Korean question; fulfilling the Geneva agreements on Indochina; outlawing weapons of mass destruction and general reduction of armaments. Peng Chen, the Mayor of Peking and member of the Communist Party Politburo, was the sole speaker on this May Day. "We must closely unite with the Soviet Union, the people's democracies and all peace-loving people of the world," he said, "and work to ease international tension and preserve peace in Asia and the world."[60]

May Day, 1952, in Tokyo began with large processions carrying red flags and banners inscribed: "No Rearmament"; "Workers, Unite for Higher Wages"; "Down with Yokida's Anti-Subversive Bill." The procession ended in Meiji Park where Norman Thomas, U.S. Socialist leader, addressed the meeting. The crowd then moved toward the Imperial Palace to voice their opposition to U.S. policy. Here, the Japanese government, following the example set by U.S. General Ridgway in 1951, had banned May Day meetings. The demonstrators, however, forced their way through and appeared upon the open Plaza facing the Emperor's Palace. The police attacked with tear gas bombs, and left one demonstrator dead and 450 wounded.[61] As late as 1955, members of the Japanese Communist Party were arrested and indicted for directing the 1952 May Day demonstrations.[62]

The chief slogan at the May Day rally in Hanoi, 1954, was "Respect the territory of Vietnam," and in English: "Independence or Death."[63] President Ho Chi Minh of the Republic of North Vietnam addressed a crowd of 90,000 at the May Day rally in Hanoi on May 1, 1957. He called for a united Vietnam and for "a fight against speculation, hoarding, corruption, and waste."[64]

In Ceylon (later Sri Lanka), May Day was made a holiday in 1956 with full pay for all Ceylonese workers, a demand of Communists and the Left for a number of years.[65]

On May 1, 1953, about 350 North Africans at Valenciennes, a French coal mining district near the Belgian border, carried the flag of "Free Algeria" in the May Day parade. French security forces were ordered to remove the flag. A battle broke out, and the police and the security troops used tear-gas and truncheons while the demonstrators hurled bricks. Thirty Africans and twenty police were hurt. Twenty arrests were made.[66]

In an effort to prevent the Algerians in Paris from making May Day the occasion for demonstrating in favor of the Algerian rebellion for independence, all demonstrations were banned on May 1, 1954.

This was repeated for the next few years; when Algerians attempted to demonstrate, calling for the triumph of democratic freedom in Algiers, they were arrested.[67] On April 24, 1958, the following report was sent from Paris to the *New York Times*: "Police Chief Maurice renewed today a ban on May Day parades to prevent street demonstrations. The ban has been in effect since 1954."[68] On May 1, 1959 about 10,000 members of the General Confederation of Labor defied a ban and staged a demonstration at the Paris Labor Exchange.[69]

On May 1, 1959, the Pope celebrated a special Mass at St. Peter's. About 40,000 workers from all over Italy were present. The London *Times* rejoiced: "By this means the subversive flavour of the holiday is displaced by a newly-unified sanctity, and Roman Catholic workers can observe it without rubbing shoulders with their Marxist colleagues."[70]

May Day demonstrations were widespread in Latin America during the 1950s. May Day, 1952, witnessed a great demonstration of support in Guatemala for progressive President Jacobo Arbenz Gutman, who was falsely branded a Communist by the United States government. Two years later, Arbenz was overthrown by a CIA-organized coup, supported by the leadership of the AFL and CIO.[71]

In the May 1, 1952 demonstration in Santiago, Chile, the workers demanded that Chilean copper mines be nationalized. "The mines are owned mostly by U.S. interests," noted the *New York Times*.[72]

In a radio broadcast on May 1, 1954, President Vargas of Brazil announced that wages in Rio de Janeiro would be doubled and increased proportionately elsewhere in the country. The decree stopped a general strike for wage increases to meet the rise in the cost of living.[73]

In 1955, the Confederation of Cuban Workers, closely linked to the AFL and dominated by dictator Fulgencio Batista, voted to ban the traditional May Day parade. But the outlawed Communist Party denounced the decision, and handbills protesting the suspension of the parade deluged the Prado promenade in Havana on April 8. Then on May 1, in defiance of the government, thousands of Havana workers tried to stage a mammoth May Day parade, but were stopped by the police. Ten women and scores of men were arrested in a struggle that lasted for hours.[74]

Four years later, following the victory of the Cuban Revolution led by Fidel Castro, Cubans marched on May Day 1959 without having to risk their lives. Noting that 500,000 marched to the Plaza de la Republica in Havana, the *New York Times* headlined the event as follows: "Cuba Holds a Massive Parade. Fatherland Or Death is the theme of the mammoth May Day Celebration."[75]

On May 3, 1954, in an editorial entitled, "The Force of Tradition," the London *Times* declared that May Day was no longer relevant. "The Socialists who chose the First of May as a day for international celebration," it declared, "belonged to an age when organized labor was often oppressed." When the workers wished to obtain an eight-hour working day or the right to vote, "there was much to be said for organized demonstration to impress their wants on the Ministers." Hence the value of May Day as a workers' holiday. "But this is no longer true. Why then go on marching?"

The World Federation of Trade Unions gave the answer in its May Day Manifesto: "The idea of unity among working people and the international trade union movement has never been so topical as now, and by marching on May Day the workers of the world can demonstrate their international solidarity against the imperialist war makers."[76]

On the eve of May 1, 1956, *New Age*, an organ of the Communist Party of South Africa, issued a statement denouncing all of the "tyrannical laws passed to take away our right to speak freely, to organise freely and struggle for citizenship rights." It continued:

> We shall demand with all the strength we have the right to govern ourselves, knowing that the workers cannot achieve economic security until they have gained political freedom.
>
> Time and the world are with us and against the oppressors. That is our Message for May Day 1956.[77]

8

To the Eve of
the Centennial

In 1960 and 1961 the New York May Day Committee was still
denied the use of Union Square for May Day; the Square continued
to be used by the Fourteenth Street Businessmen's Association for
"Union Square U.S.A." In 1961, the Labor and People's May Day
Committee was compelled to use Washington Square on May Day,
but was denied a permit for loudspeakers on the grounds that they
would interfere with classes at New York University. Nevertheless,
2,500 rallied in Washington Square and called for "Peace, Jobs,
Equality."

"May Day Lives"

With the decline of McCarthyism, the rise of struggle in the U.S.
and the development of detente between the United States and the
Soviet Union, the situation began to change. In 1962 the May Day
Committee for Defense of the Bill of Rights did obtain the use of
Union Square. Gus Hall, general secretary of the Communist Party
U.S.A., free on $10,000 bail for refusing to register under the noto-
riously vicious McCarran-Wood Act, was the main speaker. He told
the gathering that "in spite of harassment through the years ... May
Day lives and lives well as a symbol of the unity and oneness of the
common man throughout the world."[1]

The 1963 May Day rally was once again at Union Square, this time
featuring the slogans, "Hands off Cuba!" "End Segregation," and
hailing Pope John XXIII's recent peace encyclical. But the *New York
Times* emphasized only "the mild character of the rally," noting that
"the program included the singing of the 'Star Spangled Banner,'
folk songs, and addresses by college students."[2]

May Day was a powerful force during the early 1960s in the struggle against the dictatorship of Antonio de Olvara Salazar in Portugal. In 1962 and 1963, despite the government ban on May Day demonstrations, the illegal Communist Party called rallies in Lisbon and Operto. The police responded by hosing people with blue-tinted water from municipal water cans. The sprayed water marked them as demonstrators so that the police could pick them up later.[3] But thousands of Portuguese engaged in a three-hour battle with the troops and the police, many chanting "A Bastilla" ("To the Bastille"). One demonstrator was killed, but this did not stop the demonstrators calling upon the workers to protest against the rising cost of living and the "senseless war" in Angola. Thus the May Day demonstration was converted into "a main test of political strength against the Salazar regime."[4]

"U.S. Out of Vietnam"

In 1964 May Day in many countries was dedicated to ending U.S. involvement in Vietnam. At the Union Square rally in New York, Arnold Johnson, speaking for the Communist Party, called for "an end to the dirty war with Vietnam."[5] Condemnation of U.S. intervention in Vietnam overshadowed all other issues on Japan's 1965 May Day. In West Berlin, demonstrators on May 1 shouted "Leave Vietnam" as greetings from U.S. President Lyndon B. Johnson were read to the rally in Tiergarten. The demonstrators' placards read: "End the Dirty War in Vietnam!" "U.S. Out of Vietnam!"[6]

In his May Day address in Warsaw on May 1, 1965, Wladyslaw Gomulka charged the United States with having "become the policeman of colonialism" through its policies in Vietnam. He denounced the U.S. for trying "with the aid of bombs, napalm and gas to break the spirit of freedom and independence in Vietnam, and force it to its knees." The Warsaw meeting declared "We demand an immediate end to the barbarian bombing raids of the Americans in Vietnam, a stop to the daily barbarism of the United States against the Vietnamese nation and the withdrawal of American troops from South Vietnam."[7]

In Hull, England, Prime Minister Wilson was heckled when he spoke to the 1965 May Day rally and said with reference to Vietnam: "There is now after months of anxiety and worry, a little light at the end of the tunnel." The demonstrators responded by calling for the United States to withdraw immediately from South Vietnam.[8]

Banners carried in the May Day, 1966 parade in Moscow read:

"Vietnam Will Triumph" and "Bring U.S. Murderers in Vietnam to Account." In his May Day speech, Marshal Malinowsky declared: "Together with the other socialist countries we will support our Vietnamese brothers, and we are giving them and will continue to give them all possible assistance to help them defeat the foul bandit war of the United States against the heroic Vietnamese people."

On May 1, 1966, 5,000 Vietnamese in Saigon staged an anti-American demonstration about 200 yards from the U.S. Embassy. They carried posters printed in English and Vietnamese reading: "Stop the War of Race Extermination in Vietnam!" "No More Bombs!" "Americans Go Home!" A speaker demanded that the U.S. end its involvement in Vietnam, and he appealed to workers in the United States not to make any more chemical defoliants to kill crops in Vietnam. A letter was then handed to correspondents addressed to American workers urging them to play an active role in the anti-war movement in the United States. Before it ended, the meeting adopted resolutions calling for restoration of full civil liberties, including political activity, without restrictions; freedom of movement throughout the country; an end to press censorship and to the military draft; reducing the curfew; lower the cost of living; increased salaries of all workers, soldiers, and civil servants, and the right of unions to strike without permission.[9]

In 1966, the first postwar mass May Day celebration in Canada was organized in Montreal by the Comité de coordination de mouvements de gauche, set up under the cooperation of the Parti Communiste du Québec and the Parti Socialiste du Québec. Speakers representing the Confederation of National Trade Unions and the Québec Federation of Labor addressed the rally, along with speakers from the Communist and the Socialist Parties and their affiliated groups. Mass parades organized by the trade unions of Quebec took place on several May Days in the 1970s[10] (see photo, p.5).

May Day floats in Moscow in 1967 carried signs reading: "We are with you, Vietnam!" "U.S. Get out of Vietnam!" "End U.S. Aggression!" In New York's Union Square, speakers at the May Day rally called for the withdrawal of U.S. forces from Vietnam and an end to the draft. "Bring the Boys Home Alive!" "Get Out of Vietnam Now!" were the most frequent slogans on the signs carried by the demonstrators. The crowd cheered as some young men burned draft cards and chanted, "Hell, no, We Won't Go!"[11]

During the 1968 uprising of college and university students in the United States, there was more cooperation between the students and the May Day demonstrators. At the Union Square May Day rally, two Columbia University students appealed to the crowd "to support opposition to the university policies. They passed a tin can around the crowd to raise funds for a student strike against Columbia."[12]

In London, trade unionists and students marched together in the May Day parade. At the head of the marchers a trade unionist chanted "May Day is a workers' day." The students chanted slogans denouncing Enoch Powell, the racist member of Parliament who had sponsored new laws against immigrants from the West Indies and Asian countries. A group of Powell supporters, alleged to be dock workers, surged through a cordon of police to attack the anti-Powell students. But the other demonstrators came to the support of the students.[13]

President Ho Chi Minh was present at the 1968 May Day demonstration in Hanoi, but the May Day speech was delivered by Hoang Quoc Viet, president of the trade unions of North Vietnam. He charged that President Johnson's limited bombing order of March 31 was "a perfidious trick to soothe progressive opinion in the United States and the world." The following May Day, Premier Phan Van Dong (successor to Ho Chi Minh) delivered the May Day address. He declared: "Although they are very reactionary and obdurate, the United States imperialists know that they have been defeated, and are being defeated, and will surely sustain increasingly heavy defeats." He urged the United States to let "the Vietnamese people in both zones settle the problem of peaceful unification of Vietnam in accordance with their aspirations without foreign intervention."[14]

The liberation of Saigon by North Vietnam in 1975 ended the Vietnam war. The defeat of the United States was the dominant theme of many May Day demonstrations—in Moscow, Peking, Warsaw, Berlin, Sofia, Budapest, New York, London, and other cities. In Paris May Day demonstrators carried portraits of Ho Chi Minh. In Moscow, *Tass* voiced the following May Day prediction: "Sooner or later Chile's right wing Junta, the 'militarist' Israeli leadership, and 'racist' South Africa will join the overthrown Saigon regime on the rubbish dump of history."[15]

May Day in Latin America

On April 26, 1961, following the defeat of the U.S.-trained and supported counter-revolutionaries at the Bay of Pigs,* Fidel Castro

---

*In April, 1961, the United States organized a CIA-directed invasion of Cuba by counterrevolutionary Cubans at the Bay of Pigs, ninety miles from Havana. The invasion failed, and over 1,200 of the invaders were taken prisoner.

decreed that Cuba would be a "Socialist state." About 500,000 Cubans demonstrated in Havana on May Day against the "imperialistic United States" and shouted approval of the new Socialist society in Cuba. "Marchers carried slogans reading: "Viva Socialism which terminates all exploiters"; "Down with Yankee Imperialism!"; "Patria or Muerta!" Over 3,000 Cubans employed at the Guantanamo naval base (occupied by the United States since 1903) walked off the job in the first general work stoppage at the base in fifty-eight years. They joined in celebrating the establishment of Socialist Cuba and then on May 2, returned to their jobs.[16]

On May 1, 1965, in Havana, Fidel Castro denounced the invasion of the Dominican Republic by U.S. marines, calling it "one of the most criminal and shameful events in this century." Signs at the demonstration of hundreds of thousands read: "We denounce Yankee Massacre in Santo Domingo"; "Solidarity With All Peoples that are fighting Imperialism—from Vietnam to Venezuela; from the Dominican Republic to the Congo."[17]

In his 1972 May Day speech in Santiago, Chile, President Salvador Allende Gossens accused the United States of imposing an economic blockade on Chile, and pointed, among other things, to the fact that the U.S. blocked the granting of long-term development credits to Chile by international banks such as the World Bank and the Inter-American Development Bank.[18] By 1973, Allende was dead, his socialist government overthrown in a coup engineered by the CIA and U.S. corporations in conjunction with General Augusto Pinochet, who seized power.[19]

May Day demonstrations were banned under the brutal Pinochet dictatorship. A report from Chile on May 1, 1978, noted: "About 300 people were arrested in Santiago today when police dispersed a May Day demonstration which had been called in spite of government ban. Demonstrators gathered in a city Plaza and shouted 'Liberty' and 'Long Live May Day.' "[20] On the following May Day the police arrested hundreds of people trying to hold rallies. A woman told a reporter that "if the police wanted to lock up every person who was against the Government, they will have to arrest all of Chile!" The demonstrators, many of them Communists, shouted: "The people are in the street; they are calling for liberty."[21]

May Day in Other Countries

On April 25, 1974 the fascist Salazar dictatorship in Portugal was finally overthrown by an army-led uprising. On May Day, millions of Portuguese poured into the streets of Lisbon and other cities to celebrate. In 1974, Portugal celebrated its first May Day in half a century. Trade unions, political parties, civic and professional associations, led by the Socialists and Communists, marched for hours through Lisbon, then packed the sports stadium, now named "May First." Banners in the stadium read: "At Last!" and "Poetry Is In The Streets!"

The headline in the London *Times* read: "Lisbon Has a May Day to Remember." The article opened:

> Portugal has never seen a day like today, at least not for about 50 years. Hundreds of thousands of people took to the streets of Lisbon to celebrate their first legal May Day holiday and the promise of a return to democracy.... The red carnation, the symbol of Portugal's triumph over fascism, predominated. Many soldiers and sailors joined the celebrating crowds in the main march route and elsewhere throughout the city.[22]

In 1975 a military revolution in Ethiopia led by Lieutenant Colonel Mengistu Haile Mariam, overthrew the dictatorship of Emperor Haile Selassie. May Day was celebrated for the first time in Addis Ababa on May 1, 1977. A cheering crowd of 300,000 Ethiopians heard Colonel Mengistu point to "many victories" scored by the Ethiopian revolution. "The first and most historic," he added was the closing down of American institutions which were the fountains of espionage and exploitation as well as elements that diluted our culture." The cheering increased as Mengistu said that the expulsion of five U.S. agencies the previous week had ended an era of "slavery imposed by Washington."[23]

Under the Franco dictatorship, May Day in Spain was celebrated as a religious holiday—the day of Saint Joseph, the Laborer. In 1977, two years after Franco's death, the people of Madrid attempted to celebrate May Day as a workers' holiday. But the police, furious over the legalization of the Communist Party three weeks earlier and the recognition of Workers' Commissions, charged the demonstrators. Scores were injured by rubber bullets, smoke grenades, and clubs. The police even vented their anger on families picnicking in Madrid's Casa de Campo park. The reporter for the London *Times* wrote:

> I helped one young man to a first aid post after police dragged him out of his car by the hair, threw him to the ground, kicked and clubbed him—and only then asked him for his identification. They left him lying on the ground after checking his papers.[24]

Widespread protests followed, and the scene on May Day, 1978, was quite different. This time a reporter wrote:

Hundreds of thousands of Spaniards took to the streets today in the first freely celebrated May Day since Francisco Franco came to power four decades ago.

In Madrid, perhaps 300,000 people took part in a parade organized jointly by the Communist and Socialist unions. They marched in the rain under red banners, first to the Prado museum, then to the towering Puerto de Alcalo, where speakers urged unity of the left.

"Unity! Unity!" shouted the soaked throng gathered around the 10th century triumphal arch. About a million people were reported to have demonstrated across the country.[25]

At least 36 persons were killed and about 299 wounded at a giant May Day rally on May 1, 1977 at Taksim Square in the heart of Istanbul, Turkey. The rally was organized by the leftist group known as DISK, one of the two big labor federations in Turkey.[26] On May Day, 1979, more than 1,000 persons were arrested in Istanbul when they tried to hold rallies in defiance of martial law. The leaders of DISK had planned a march to Taksim Square to honor those killed on May Day, 1977. Ten of the leaders of Turkey's second largest labor federation were arrested. Outside of Istanbul another 700 people were arrested for ignoring the 29-hour May Day curfew.[27]

Tens of thousands of Iranians marched through the streets of Tehran on May 1, 1979 "in a kind of labor celebration that the Shah had banned." The demonstrators ranged from Moslem fundamentalist followers of Ayatolleh Khomeni to Communists. The May Day call had been issued by leftist groups, including the Tudeh (Communist) Party, and was supported by the Fedaijeem, the Marxist guerrillas. It was taken up by the religious revolutionary leadership. There were two separate rallies, however; the leftist rally joined by many of the unemployed, of 100,000, and the Islamic rally of 30,000.[28]

On April 4, 1979, *Neue Deutschland*, the official Party organ of the German Democratic Republic, published in Berlin, issued its May Day Manifesto. It included 56 issues, among them the following:

- Long live the first of May, the day of struggle of the International Working Class.
- Greetings to workers of all lands on May 1.
- Under the banner of Marxism-Leninism to new advances in the struggle for Peace and Socialism.
- Long live the Socialist Fatherland—the DDR!
- Brotherly greetings to the Soviet People, and their powerful representative—the Communist Party of the Soviet Union.
- We greet the people of the Socialist brotherlands.
- The stronger Socialism the surer the peace!
- For the 30th anniversary of the DDR—good quality of work—higher levels of production!

- Our brotherly greetings to the fighters for national and social liberation in Africa, Asia and Latin America.
- Our greetings of solidarity to the anti-fascist fighters in Chile, Uruguay, and the other Latin American countries.
- Solidarity greetings to the people of Angola, Mozambique, Ethiopia, Afghanistan and all countries in Africa and Asia.
- Solidarity with the Arab people in their struggle for justice and freedom in the Near East.
- Solidarity with the Palestinian people and the PLO in their struggle for Peace and Self-Determination.
- Solidarity with the people of Zimbabwe, Namibia and South Africa in their struggle against Colonialism, Racism, and Apartheid for freedom and national liberation.
- Long live the international proletariat; Long live the 1st of May 1979.[29]

"Millions of people took part in May Day parades throughout the world yesterday," observed the London *Daily Telegraph* on May 2, 1979. Not many of these demonstrations were in the United States. By the early 1970s, the Left regained the use of New York's Union Square for the annual May Day celebration. But there were still no parades, and the attendance at the rally was small by former standards. In 1971 the *New York Times* reported that a few hundred persons attended the "traditional May Day gathering," carrying banners with the slogans "End the War in Indochina," and "Free Angela Davis."[30]* The number at the 1973 Union Square rally had increased, to 800 persons according to the *Times*, which added: "Those in the audience, most of them older people, heard speeches on the themes of corruption in the Nixon Administration, the struggle against capitalism, the farm workers' fight and welfare reform."[31]

Rebuilding May Day—U.S.A.!

The small number of participants in U.S. May Day demonstrations produced the following question and answer, published in the *Daily World* (successor to the *Daily Worker*) on the eve of May Day, 1978. Henry North of Jamaica, New York, asked: "An old timer on my job told me that there used to be huge May Day parades in this country. Why is May Day today such a big event in other parts of the world

---

*Angela Davis, dismissed as Assistant Professor of Philosophy at the University of California, Los Angeles, for membership in the Communist Party, was later charged with kidnapping, conspiracy, and murder in connection with an attempted prison break in California. At her trial in 1972, Ms. Davis acted as her own counsel and won a verdict of not guilty.

but not here?" Irving Herman, Coordinator, Committee for a United Labor and People's May Day, replied that in "the 1930s, 1940s and the early 1950s, New York witnessed massive May Day parades and rallies involving tens of thousands, including the participation of many unions. The May Day of those years reflected the powerful upsurge of the working class and the people during the Depression, World War II and the immediate post-war years." However, with the advent of the Cold War, Herman continued, the hysteria of Mc-Carthyism, passage of the Taft-Hartley law, the disruption of the Left-Center coalition in the CIO, and the expulsion from the CIO of the unions under Left and progressive leadership, the "former broad character of May Day fell victim . . ." But a new situation had emerged in the mid-1970s, reflected in the rank-and-file upsurge in steel, the militancy of the coal miners, and the spirit of struggle among many American workers. "Under these conditions, the possibilities exist to rebuild May Day." He concluded:[32]

> A large, enthusiastic united front May Day this year will help hasten the day when organized labor itself, particularly that sector under more progressive leadership, will once again assume the leadership in promoting May Days with a strong labor participation.

In its May Day statement of 1977,* the Central Committee of the Communist Party USA. called for a 30-hour week at no cut in pay. "The need for a shorter work week has once again come to the fore," it declared. "Under capitalism technological advances result in fewer jobs. Thus unemployment, which is a constant feature of capitalist society, now remains at a high rate. Many of the 10 million unemployed are youth, particularly Black, Chicano and Puerto Rican. At the same time, conditions of work have become hazardous to life and limb, with industrial accidents and occupational diseases taking an increasing toll. The time is therefore overripe for another major reduction in the work week."[33]

The Left did make a renewed effort in 1978 "to rebuild May Day," with the first parade in New York City in many years held on Saturday April 29, "to accommodate workers who cannot take off Monday,

---

*The May Day statement made the additional point that although May Day was born in the United States, "the corporate rulers of this country and their paid lackeys try their damndest to get us to forget and renounce our proud roots. They want us to believe that May Day is some kind of foreign holiday to be scorned and rejected by U.S. labor. Toward this end they have named the first of May, 'loyalty day.' What they mean is loyalty to Big Business and its right to rule the roost in the interests of its ever greater profits." (*Daily World*, April 30, 1977.)

May 1st, to celebrate labor's traditional holiday."[34] The marchers assembled at Tompkins Square at 1:00 p.m., and, led by the labor contingent, organized by local officers and rank-and-filers from seventeen unions, proceeded to Union Square for a 2:30 p.m. rally featuring speakers and entertainment. The United Labor and People's May Day Committee expressed the hope that the participation of the labor contingent "can spearhead the drive to encourage official labor participation in the organization of future May Days."[35]

A wide variety of issues were advanced in May Day celebrations throughout the world during the 1980s. In Moscow, slogans proclaimed: "No to the Aggressive Nuclear Strategy of the United States!" "No to Medium-Range Nuclear Missiles in Europe!" "No to War!"[36] Along with these issues, the key issue in England was unemployment. On May 1, 1981, the "people's march for jobs" left Liverpool on its 280-mile walk to London to demand work for the unemployed.[37] In the United States, in New York, Chicago, Detroit, San Francisco, Boston, and other cities, the People's Fightback against Reaganism was the central theme of the 1982 May Day parades and rallies. The New York Committee for a United Labor and People's May Day listed the following issues in its May Day Manifesto:[38]

- Jobs or Unemployment Insurance for all Jobless.
- Support for labor's struggles against giveback and takeaway contracts.
- Restore the Reagan-Koch* budget cuts of essential social programs.
- Advance the fight against racism and for affirmative action.**
- Slash the military budget and end the suicidal arms race.
- Solidarity with people's fighting for freedom and national independence. Put an end to U.S. intervention in El Salvador.

Peace and Shorter Hours

At May Day meetings in the Federal Republic of Germany on May 1, 1983, the main stress was on the campaign against deployment of nuclear weapons. At the same time, trade union leaders urged the Government to shorten the work week and introduce a job-creation program to ease rising unemployment. "A shorter working week should become a demand workers can go on strike for," Ernst

---

*The reference is to the policies directed against the poor by President Ronald Reagan and New York Mayor Edward Koch.
**Affirmative Action involves programs to make it easier for Blacks, other minorities and women to gain entry to universities, jobs, etc. that had been closed to them in the past.

Haar, leader of the Railway Workers' Union, declared in his May Day speech.[39]

The call "to end the suicidal arms race" was also echoed in May Day demonstrations throughout Europe in 1982 and 1983. Along with this was the demand for a restoration of detente between the United States and the Soviet Union, and the abandonment of the new Cold War policies of the Reagan Administration.

On May Day, 1984, trade union leaders warned Chancellor Kohl of the Federal Republic of Germany that there would be strikes if their demands for a shorter work week were ignored.[40] When this warning was ignored, the workers did go out on strike. After six weeks, the metalworkers union won a 38½ hour week without a cut in pay and pledged to continue the struggle to reduce the work week to 35 hours. In Denmark, a general strike for shorter hours took place early in 1985, and the Canadian trade union movement made shorter hours the main issue, as did workers in South America.[41]

In the late 1970s and early 1980s the All Union Committee for the Shorter Work Week sparked an educational campaign in the United States for labor action and pressed Congress to pass the shorter work week bill introduced by Representative John Conyers of Michigan. On the eve of May Day, 1985, Conyers reintroduced the Shorter Work Week bill of 1985 which included: "(1) A reduction of statutory work week to 32 hours; (2) A prohibition of forced overtime, and (3) An increase in pay for overtime from time-and-a-half to double-time."[42]

Thus as the centennial of May Day approached, the shorter work week again emerged, along with peace and disarmament as major demands of the struggle.

Five hundred trade unionists celebrated May Day in Boston on May 1, 1985, with a picket line and rally in solidarity with the workers of South Africa. The picket line, several blocks long, surrounded Deak-Perera Co., the major supplier of South African Krugerands (gold coins) in the Boston area. Prior to the picketing, several trade unionists sat in at Deak-Perera and became locked in for the evening. Among the unions represented were United Steel Workers of America Local 8751, International United Electrical Workers Local 201, United Food and Commercial Workers Union Local 616, and Hotel and Restaurant Employees Union Local 26.[43]

The leaflet distributed at the demonstration was headed: "May 1st. A Day of International Labor Solidarity with South African Workers." It continued:

May Day poster, SACTU, 1985

On May 1, 1886 ... U.S. workers demonstrated for the 8 hour day, trade union rights, justice and dignity. May 1st is now celebrated as a day of International Solidarity all over the world!

On May 1, 1985 ... almost 100 years later, South African workers are still fighting for their freedom! The South African apartheid system denies black workers their basic trade union rights.

PICKET AND RALLY![44]

The rally that followed the picketing emphasized two themes: (1) international solidarity with South African workers against apartheid, and (2) revive May 1 as the holiday of U.S. workers.[45]

The second theme of the rally was also featured in the May Day, 1985 issue of *Labor Today*, the militant monthly published in Chicago. Editor Fred Gaboury urged workers in the United States to recapture the historic meaning of May Day and couple it with the current struggle for a shorter work week and workers' rights:

The struggles of nearly a century ago have had tremendous impact on workers around the world and continue today. Workers the world over stand in solidarity on May Day. The time has come for U.S. workers to reclaim this holiday as part of their history and join with others regenerating the spirit of the first May Day and the fight for shorter hours and labor rights.[46]

"Reclaim May Day!" Will Parry appealed in the same issue of *Labor Today*. Parry pointed out that from the inception of May Day, the U.S. corporate power structure had sought "to falsify its significance and to make its observance impossible in the land of its birth." Their major tactic had been red-baiting: "May Day, born in the USA thirty-one years before the October Revolution in the USSR, is presented as though it had been secretly hatched in the Kremlin. It is portrayed as something alien to the struggles of the very working class that gave it birth." In place of May Day, U.S. workers were offered "Loyalty Day" and "Law Day" by "people who invented loyalty oaths" and who "cynically flaunt the nation's labor laws."

"Surely it is time, and past time, for the working people of our country to reclaim their significant May Day heritage.

"Let May 1, 1986, mark the rebirth of the observance of May Day in cities across our country—across the land whose labor movement created this mighty holiday and gave it to the workers of the whole world."[47]

In a number of cities, including New York, San Francisco, Seattle, Milwaukee and Chicago, plans got under way to "reclaim May Day" on the Centennial of the first May Day at Haymarket Square. In

Chicago, more than fifty community, cultural, labor and religious groups came together and formed the Haymarket Centennial Committee to prepare a month-long celebration of the 100th anniversary of May Day and the Haymarket martyrs.

Among the events planned for May Day, 1986, are conferences on labor history, concerts with folk and ethnic musicians, film and video festivals, exhibits and mass rallies. In its call the committee said: "The Haymarket Centennial gives us a chance to correct the misrepresentation of history and reclaim our history and culture." The committee's call urged massive support for the 1986 commemoration, making it "a celebration of the struggles of the workers everywhere for peace, justice and equality, as well as democratic rights on the job."[48]

As far back as May, 1951, at the height of the Cold War, Gus Hall, then National Secretary of the Communist Party of the United States, expressed a wish and voiced a prediction. "Some day," he wrote, "all the people of the United States will proudly hail and understand that which today only a minority does—what a great honor May Day is to our working class." He looked forward to the time when "the working class of the U.S.A. will be in a position to make this day—May Day—that started in support of the struggle for the eight-hour day, a legal holiday celebrated by all the people of the United States."[49]

It is to be hoped that the centennial of May Day—May 1, 1986—will witness the launching of a vigorous campaign to achieve this goal. Then once again the workers of the United States will observe a world Labor Day together with their brothers and sisters throughout the world. In the words of the Milan correspondent of May 1, 1890, the first international May Day:

On this day laborers all over the world should feel the unity of their class as a bond superior to all others, and should give peaceable expression to that feeling in taking a holiday and demonstrating.[50]

Notes

Introduction

1. *Fourth Annual Report*, Bureau of Labor Statistics, New York, 1887, p. 8
2. William J. Walsh *Curiosities of Popular Customs*, Philadelphia, 1898, p. 606
3. Eugene P. Link, *Democratic-Republican Societies*, 1790–1800, New York, 1942, p. 242
4. For examples of the rewritten Declarations of Independence, *see* Philip S. Foner, editor, *We the Other People: Alternative Declarations of Independence by Labor Groups, Farmers, Women's Rights Advocates, Socialists, and Blacks, 1829–1975*, Urbana, Ill., 1975.
5. New York *Daily Sentinel*, July 12, 1829
6. Peter J. McGuire has usually been credited with making the first formal suggestion for Labor Day in a speech before the Central Labor Union of New York City in May 1882. As a result, McGuire, leader of the United Brotherhood of Carpenters and Joiners, co-founder and leading official of the American Federation of Labor, and, at one time, a Socialist associated with the Lassallean wing of the movement, has been called the "Father of Labor Day." However, recently that title has been bestowed upon Matthew Maguire, secretary of the Machinists and Blacksmiths' local of Brooklyn, New York, organizer of the Central Labor Union of New York City, victorious candidate for alderman in Paterson, New Jersey, on the Socialist Labor Party ticket in 1894, and SLP candidate for governor of New Jersey and vice-president of the United States. Each of these two men has his champions, but more credit recently has been given to Maguire than to McGuire. (*See* Jonathan Grossman, "Who is the Father of Labor Day?" *Labor History* 14 [Fall, 1973]: 622–23).
7. *Truth*, August 7, 28, 1882; *Irish World*, August 5, 12, 1882
8. *Journal of United Labor*, June 25, 1884; *John Swinton's Paper*, August 31, 1884
9. *Proceedings*, Federation of Organized Trades and Labor Unions, 1884 Convention, p. 23
10. Grossman, p. 621
11. Ibid., pp. 621–22
12. *American Federationist*, 1 (August, 1894): 128–29
13. Walsh, pp. 535–43

Chapter 1

1. *Daily Worker*, May 1, 1955
2. Ibid.; Alexander Trachtenberg, *History of May Day*, New York, 1929, revised, 1947, p. 3

3. Philip S. Foner, *History of the Labor Movement in the United States* 1 (New York, 1947): 100–103
4. Ibid., pp. 106–107
5. Ibid., pp. 115–18
6. Ibid., p. 118
7. Ibid., p. 163
8. Philip S. Foner, ed., *The Factory Girls*, Urbana, Illinois, 1975, pp. 213–70
9. Ibid., pp. 233, 269–70
10. Foner, *Labor History* 1: 217–18
11. *Mechanics' Free Press*, June 21, 1828
12. Foner, *Labor History* 1: 363–65
13. Karl Marx, *Capital* 1 (New York, 1937): 309
14. *Labor Standard*, June 9, 1878
15. Ira Steward, *Poverty*, Boston, n.d.; Dorothy W. Douglas, "Ira Steward on Consumption and Unemployment," *Journal of Political Economy* 40 (August, 1932): 532–40; Hyman Kuritz, "Ira Steward and the Eight-Hour Day," *Science & Society* 20 (Spring, 1956): 118–22
16. Ira Steward, "Political Economy of Eight Hours," n.d., State Historical Society of Wisconsin
17. David Roediger, *Joseph Weydemeyer: Articles on the Eight-Hour Movement*, Chicago, 1978, pp. 1–3
18. Foner, *Labor History* 1: 374
19. Karl Marx, *Capital* 1: 301
20. Foner, *Labor History* 1: 374; John R. Commons and Associates, eds., *A Documentary History of the American Industrial Society* 14 (Cleveland, 1910): 139–40
21. Foner, *Labor History* 1: 377; Mary Cahill, *Shorter Hours*, New York, 1932, p. 148
22. Foner, *Labor History* 1: 379
23. Ibid., pp. 379–80
24. *National Workman*, Feb. 2, 1867; *Workingman's Advocate*, Feb. 20, March 13, 1871
25. Cahill, p. 148
26. Felicia Johnson Deyrup, *Arms Makers of the Connecticut Valley*, Northampton, Mass., 1948, pp. 206–207; Ohio Bureau of Labor Statistics, *Second Annual Report*, Columbus, 1879, pp. 267–90; David Montgomery, *Beyond Equality: Labor and the Radical Republicans, 1862–1872*, (New York, 1967) pp. 319–20; Cahill, p. 70; Foner, *Labor History* 1: 378
27. Montgomery, pp. 321–23; Cahill, pp. 70–71
28. Montgomery, pp. 387–402; Foner, *Labor History* 1: 420–32
29. *John Swinton's Paper*, Nov. 18, 1883, April 6, 1884; United States Commissioner of Labor, *First Annual Report*, Washington, D.C., 1886, p. 226
30. Foner, *Labor History* 1: 509–11; Philip S. Foner, *History of the Labor Movement in the United States* 2: (New York, 1955) 47–63
31. Foner, *Labor History* 2: 55
32. Terence V. Powderly, *Thirty Years of Life and Labor, 1859–1889*, Columbus, Ohio, 1890, pp. 85–86
33. Cahill, p. 47
34. Ibid., p. 43; Terence V. Powderly, "The Plea for Eight Hours," *North American Review* 150 (April, 1890): 465–69
35. Norman J. Ware, *The Labor Movement in the United States, 1860–1895*, New York, 1929, p. 303; Powderly, *Thirty Years*, pp. 480–83
36. Foner, *Labor History* 1: 512–24
37. *Proceedings*, Federation of Organized Trades and Labor Unions of the United States and Canada, 1881, p. 19, (FOTLU)
38. *Proceedings*, FOTLU, 1882, p. 218; 1883, p. 16
39. Cahill, pp. 48–49; Samuel Gompers, *Seventy Years of Life and Labor*, New York,

1925, 1: 72; Bernard Mandel, *Samuel Gompers: A Biography*, Yellow Springs, 1963, pp. 52–53; Philip S. Foner, "Marx's *Capital* in the United States," *Science & Society* 31 (Fall, 1967): 461–66

40. *Proceedings*, FOTLU, 1882, p. 19; *John Swinton's Paper*, April 4, 1886
41. *Proceedings*, FOTLU, 1884, pp. 10–14, 24–25; Foner, *Labor History*, 2: 98
42. *Proceedings*, FOTLU, 1884, pp. 8, 10–14
43. *John Swinton's Paper*, Oct. 26, 1884.
44. Foner, *Labor History* 1: 202, 209
45. *Workingman's Advocate*, April 24, 1875
46. Montgomery, pp. 306–308; *Boston Daily Evening Voice*, May 2,4, 1867
47. Powderly, *Thirty Years*, p. 482
48. Ibid., pp. 483–85; Foner, *Labor History* 2: 100
49. Powderly, *Thirty Years*, p. 253; Brotherhood of Carpenters & Joiners to Terence V. Powderly, November 21, 1885, Terence V. Powderly Papers, Catholic University of America
50. *Proceedings*, FOTLU, 1885, pp. 11–15; Printed "Appeal to all Trade and Labor Unions," February 1, 1886, copy in American Federation Archives, Washington, D.C. Hereinafter cited as AFL Archives
51. Henry David, *The History of the Haymarket Affair*, New York, 1936, p. 164
52. Powderly, *Thirty Years*, p. 496; Ware, pp. 310–13
53. *John Swinton's Paper*, April 11, 1886; *Chicago Tribune*, April 11, 1886
54. Eunice Minette Schuster, *Native-American Anarchism: A Study of Left-Wing American Individualism*, Northampton, Mass., 1931–32, pp. 162–64
55. Richard T. Ely, *The Labor Movement in America*, New York, 1886, pp. 358–64; David, pp. 83–101
56. Morris Hillquit, *History of Socialism in the United States*, New York, 1965, pp. 220–24
57. David, pp. 166–67; Mandel, pp. 52–53; Jeremy Brecher, *Strike!* Greenwich, Conn., 1974, pp. 68–70
58. *John Swinton's Paper*, April 18, 1886
59. Wisconsin Bureau of Labor and Industrial Statistics, *Biennial Reports for 1885–1886*, p. 319
60. *John Swinton's Paper*, April 11, 1886
61. Foner, *Labor History* 2: 97; George Gunton, *Wealth and Progress*, New York, 1887, p. 243; *John Swinton's Paper*, May 16, 1886
62. Charles E. Endicott, *Capital and Labor. Address before the Central Trades Union, Boston, March 28, 1886*, Boston, n.d., p. 11
63. Philip S. Foner, *American Labor Songs of the Nineteenth Century*, Urbana, Ill., 1975, pp. 581–82
64. Boston *Herald*, April 26, 1886, reprinted in Jama Lazeron, " 'The Workingman's Hour': The 1886 Labor Uprising in Boston," *Labor History* 21 (Spring, 1980): 202

Chapter 2

1. *John Swinton's Paper*, May 8, 1886; Brecher, *Strike!*, pp. 66–67; *Bradstreets*, May 8,15, 1886
2. *New York Times*, May 2–5, 1886
3. William J. Adelman, *Haymarket Revisited*, Chicago, 1976, p. 15; *John Swinton's Paper*, May 8, 1886; *New York Times*, May 2, 1886; *Chicago Tribune*, May 2, 1886
4. New York *Sun*, May 2, 1886
5. *New York Times*, May 2, 1886; New York *Herald*, May 2, 1886; Mandel, *Samuel Gompers*, p. 54
6. New York *Sun*, May 2, 1886

7. Leon Fink, *Workingmen's Democracy: The Knights of Labor and American Politics*, Urbana, Ill., 1983, p. 190; Milwaukee *Journal*, May 2, 1886
8. *Cleveland Gazette*, May 8, 1886; Philip S. Foner, *Organized Labor and the Black Worker*, 1619–1981, New York, 1981, p. 50
9. Boston *Evening Transcript*, May 2–6, 1886
10. Chicago *Tribune*, May 4, 1886
11. *John Swinton's Paper*, May 15, 1886
12. Thomas W. Gavett, *Development of the Labor Movement in Milwaukee*, Madison and Milwaukee, 1965, pp. 57–69; St. Louis *Post-Dispatch*, May 3–4, 1886; Brecher, pp. 69–76
13. *John Swinton's Paper*, May 9, 1886; Brecher, p. 72
14. David, *History of Haymarket Affair*, pp. 187–91; Brecher, p. 76
15. David, pp. 187–91; Foner, *Labor History* 2: 105
16. David, pp. 191–92, 196; "Story of the McCormick Massacre," *Daily Worker*, April 29, 1936
17. David, pp. 194, 196; Chicago *Inter-Ocean*, May 4, 1886
18. David, pp. 198–205; Foner, *Labor History* 2: 106–107; Brecher, P. 76
19. Paul Avrich, *The Haymarket Tragedy*, Princeton, N.J., 1984, pp. 88–90
20. Avrich, pp. 78–80
21. Chicago *Mail*, May 1, 1886
22. *Journal of the Illinois Historical Society*, December, 1938, p. 204; see also *John Swinton's Paper*, May 16, 1886
23. David, pp. 206–32
24. Cincinnati *Enquirer*, May 6, 1886; Cincinnati *Times-Star*, May 5–6, 1886
25. Milwaukee *Journal*, May 3–5, 1886; Gavett, pp. 63–64; Wisconsin Bureau of Labor and Industrial Statistics, *Report*, 1885–1886, p. 322
26. Milwaukee *Journal*, May 5–6, 1886
27. Ibid., May 7, 1886; Wisconsin Bureau of Labor and Industrial Statistics, *Report*, 1885–1886, pp. 341–42
28. Boston *Evening Transcript*, May 9–10, 1886
29. James M. Morris, "No Haymarket for Cincinnati," *Ohio History* 83 (1974); *Bradstreets*, May 8, 1886; *John Swinton's Paper*, May 2,9, 1886; *Proceedings*, AFL Convention, 1886, p. 6
30. *Report of the Industrial Commission on the Relations of Capital and Labor Employed in Manufactures and General Business* 7 (Washington, D.C., 1901): 603
31. *Proceedings*, AFL Convention, 1889, p. 42
32. David, pp. 223–28
33. J.P. Altgeld, *Reasons for Pardoning Fielden, Neebe, and Schwab*, Springfield, Ill., 1896, p. 8
34. David, pp. 258–60
35. Avrich, pp. 118–20
36. Altgeld, pp. 12–14
37. David, pp. 253–54, 297–300; Foner, *Labor History* 2: 109
38. Manuscript notebook of Albert R. Parsons, Albert R. Parsons Papers, State Historical Society of Wisconsin
39. David, pp. 315–27, 446–47
40. Ibid., p. 489
41. *Famous Speeches of the Eight Chicago Anarchists in Court*, Chicago, 1910, pp. 20–24
42. Ibid., pp. 40–43
43. Foner, *Labor History* 2: 111–12
44. Samuel Gompers, *Seventy Years . . .* 1: 187
45. Philip S. Foner, ed., *Autobiographies of the Haymarket Martyrs*, New York, 1975, p. 12
46. *Proceedings*, AFL Convention, 1886, pp. 46, 100–08

47. Foner, *Labor History* 2: 112
48. David, pp. 388, 397–98; *New York Tribune*, Nov. 6, 1887
49. *The Commonweal*, Oct. 27, 1887, p. 340; *Freedom*, November, 1887, p. 56; David, p. 426
50. Executive Clemency Files, Illinois State Archives, Springfield, Illinois
51. Ibid.
52. Avrich, pp. 287–89
53. David, pp. 479–507
54. Adelman, p. 23
55. Ibid., p. 24
56. Ibid., p. 25
57. Altgeld, pp. 18–20
58. Foner, *Labor History* 2: 114; David, pp. 499–500; Clippings in Labadie Collection, classified under the head of "Haymarket," University of Michigan

Chapter 3

1. Printed Circular issued by AFL Executive Council, New York, January 19, 1889, *AFL Corr*; Samuel Gompers to H. J. Skeffington, Jan. 3, 1889; Gompers to John O'Brien, Feb. 7, 1889, Samuel Gompers Letter-Books, Library of Congress, Manuscripts Division. Hereinafter cited as GLB
2. "A Ringing Eight-Hour Call, Practical Suggestions by President Gompers," *AFL Corr.*; Gompers to the officers and delegates of the General Assembly of the K. of L., November 9, 1889, GLB
3. George Gunton, *The Economic and Social Importance of the Eight-Hour Movement*, Washington, D.C., 1889
4. Lewis Lorwin, *Labor and Internationalism*, New York, 1929, pp. 66–67
5. *Protokol des Internationalen Arbeiter-Congresses*, 1889, p. 11; Philip S. Foner, ed., *Clara Zetkin: Selected Writings*, New York, 1984, p. 23
6. Gompers, *Seventy Years* 1: 66–67; Gompers to August Keufer, January 10, 1889; Gompers to Andrew Gely, May 29, 1889, GLB
7. Gompers to Andrew Gely, May 29, 1889; Gompers to Victor Delahaye, May 31, 1893, GLB. "May Day," *American Federationist* 1 (May, 1894): 52
8. *Protokol des Internationalen Arbeiter-Congresses*, 1889, p. 123
9. Eric Haas, *The Socialist Labor Party and the Internationals*, New York, 1949, p. 34; Boris Reinstein, *International May Day and American Labor Day*, New York, 1915, p. 9; David, p. 540
10. Sidney Fine, "Is May Day American in Origin?" *Historian* 16 (Spring, 1954): 121–34
11. Gabriell Deville, "Historique du Premier Mai," *Le Devenir Social* 2 (Avril, 1896): 306–08; Fine, p. 132
12. Fine, pp. 133–34
13. Gompers to James H. Perry, January 22, 1889; Gompers to John O'Brien, Feb. 7, 1889, GLB
14. Eleanor Marx Aveling and W. Thorne to Gompers, Jan. 5, 1891, *AFL Corr.*
15. Foner, *Labor History* 2: 180–81; Sidney Fine, "The Eight Hour Movement in the United States, 1888–1891," *Mississippi Valley Historical Review* 11 (December, 1953): 441–43
16. Gompers to the Officers and delegates of the General Assembly of the Knights of Labor, Atlanta, Georgia, Nov. 9, 1889, GLB.; Powderly to John W. Hayes, Dec. 16, 1889, Terence V. Powderly-John W. Hayes Correspondence, Catholic University of America
17. Gompers to P. J. McGuire, March 20, 1890; Gompers to the Toilers of America, April 28, 1890, GLB
18. Louisville *Courier-Journal*, May 2, 1890; *New York Times*, May 2, 1890

19. Chicago *Tribune*, May 2, 1890
20. New York *Sun*, May 2, 1890; New York *World*, May 2, 1890
21. Gompers to the editor of *Labor Tribune*, July 26, 1890, GLB; Fine, "Eight-Hour Movement," p. 455; *Bradstreets*, May 3, 10, 31, 1890; Gompers to Emil Applehagen, Sept. 18, 1890, GLB
22. Ryujo Komatsu and Ichiro Saga, "First May Day in Japan," Paper delivered at Conference on "The First May Day Throughout the World," Second Congress of the World Association of Institutes for the Study of the History of the Labor Movement, Mexico, 1980, pp. 1–2. Reprinted in Spanish in Enrique Suarez Gaona, ed., *El Primer 1⁰ de Mayo en el Mundo* 2: (Mexico City, 1982): 119–20
23. Dieter Fricke, "The First Decade of Mayday Celebrations in the German Working Class Movement," Paper delivered at Second Congress of World Association of Institutes for the Study of the History of the Labor Movement, Mexico City, 1980, pp. 1–2; August Bebel, *Briefwechsel mit Friedrich Engels*, Hrsg. Werner Blumenberg, Amsterdam, 1965, p. 384
24. Karl Marx and Frederick Engels, *Letters to Americans 1848–1895: A Selection*, New York, 1953, p. 231
25. Fricke, pp. 3–4
26. Ibid., p. 5
27. Ibid., pp. 2–3
28. Dieter Fricke, *Kleine Geschichte des Ersten Mai*, Berlin, 1980, pp. 35–38
29. Fricke, "The First Decade," pp. 8–9
30. Dieter Fricke, *Die Deutsche Arbeiterbewegung 1869–1914. Ein Handbuch über hire Organisation and Tatigkeit in Klassenkampf*, Berlin, 1976, pp. 666–72
31. August Bebel, "Die Maifeier und Ihre Bedeutung," *Die Neue* Zeit 11 (1892/1893): 439; Fricke, *Kleine Geschichte*, pp. 40–42
32. Ottile Baader, *Ein steiniger Weg. Lebenserinnerungen*, Stuttgart, Berlin, 1921, p. 28
33. Herbert Steiner, "The First May Day in Austria," Paper delivered at Conference on "The First May Day Throughout the World," Second Congress of the World Association of Institutes for the Study of the History of the Labor Movement, Mexico, 1980, pp. 1–2
34. *Neue Freie Presse*, May 1, 1890; reprinted in London *Times*, May 2, 1890
35. Steiner, pp. 7–8
36. *Neue Freie Presse*, May 1,2, 1890
37. Steiner, pp. 2–3
38. Ibid., p. 3
39. *Arbeiter-Zeitung*, May 8, 1890
40. Quoted in Steiner, p. 4
41. Tibor Erényi, "Hungria Primero de Mayo, 1890," *El Primer 1⁰ de Mayo en el Mundo* 2:103–18
42. London *Times*, May 2, 1890
43. Ervin Pamlenyi, editor, *A History of Hungary*, Corvida, 1973, p. 371; Ereny, pp. 117–18
44. Irena Koberdowa, "The First May Day Celebrations in Poland in 1890," Paper delivered at conference on "The First May Day Throughout the World," pp. 1–3
45. Ibid., p. 3
46. *Robotnik*, Lwow, April 1, 1890, in Koberdowa, pp. 5–6
47. Ibid., p. 7
48. Ibid., p. 8
49. Ibid., pp. 9–10
50. Ibid., pp. 11–12
51. Ibid., p. 12
52. Ibid., pp. 12–13
53. Ibid., pp. 14–17

54. London *Times*, May 5, 1890
55. Yvonne Kapp, *Eleanor Marx* 2 (New York, 1976): 375–78; George Copsey to Samuel Gompers, Feb. 1, 1890, AFL Correspondence.
56. London *Times*, May 2, 1890
57. Ibid.
58. Ibid.
59. A. Markus and J. Merritt, "Australia's First May Day," Paper delivered at Conference on "The First May Day Throughout the World," pp. 1–2
60. Ibid., pp. 4–5
61. Ibid., pp. 9–11
62. Ibid., pp. 11–12
63. Ibid., pp. 14–15; Leon Fox, "Early Australian May Days," *Labour History*, May, 1962, pp. 36–42
64. Philip S. Foner, *A History of Cuba and its Relations with the United States* 2 (New York, 1963): 302–03
65. Fabio Grobart, "El Primero de 1⁰ de mayo en Cuba," Paper delivered at conference on "The First May Day Throughout the World," pp. 3–5
66. *New York Times*, May 2, 1890
67. Grobart, pp. 13–15
68. Ibid., p. 16; Foner, *History of Cuba* 2: 305
69. Quoted in Steiner, p. 3
70. Preface to the 4th German edition of *The Communist Manifesto*, dated May 1, 1890, in *The Communist Manifesto of K. Marx and* F. Engels, New York, 1930, p. 268; Foner, *Labor History* 2: 182

Chapter 4

1. London *Times*, May 3, 1891
2. *The People*, April 26, 1891
3. Ibid.
4. McAlister Coleman, *Men and Coal*, New York, 1943, pp. 54–55
5. *Proceedings*, AFL Convention, 1891, p. 47; Gompers, *Seventy Years*, 1: 307–09; *The People*, May 3, 1891
6. *Proceedings*, AFL Convention, 1891, pp. 12–13; *New York Times*, May 2, 1891
7. *New York Times*, May 10, 1891
8. Chicago *Daily News*, May 2, 1891
9. Boston *Herald*, April 26,30, May 2, 1891; *The People*, April 26, 1891
10. *The People*, April 26, 1891
11. *New York Times*, May 2, 1891; *The People*, April 26, 1891
12. *New York Times*, May 2, 1891
13. *The People*, April 26, 1891
14. Fricke, "The First Decade of May Day in the German Working Class Movement," p. 8
15. Frederick Engels to Paul Lafargue, in Marx Engels, *Werke*, vol. 38, p. 27
16. Fricke, p. 8
17. London *Times*, May 4,5, 1891
18. Ibid.
19. *The People*, April 26, 1891
20. London *Times*, May 2, 1891
21. Ibid.
22. *The People*, April 26, 1891
23. *New York Times*, May 2, 1891; London *Times*, May 2, 1891
24. *New York Times*, May 5, 1891
25. Ervin Pamlényi, editor, *A History of Hungary*, Corvinia, 1973, pp. 371–72
26. Fricke, p. 8

27. *The People*, May 3,10, 1891; Kapp, p. 474
28. Kapp, p. 475
29. Ibid.
30. London *Times* May 4, 1891
31. Ibid.
32. Ibid.
33. Markus and Merritt, pp. 14–15
34. Silvia Regina Ferraz Petersen "El Primer 1⁰· de Mayo en Brasil," in *El Primer 1⁰ de Mayo en el Mundo*, vol. I, pp. 41–42
35. *New York Times*, April 28-May 1, 1892
36. *The People*, May 8, 1892
37. London *Times*, May 2, 1892; *The People*, May 8, 1892
38. London *Times*, May 2, 1892
39. Ibid.
40. Ibid.
41. Ibid.
42. *The People*, May 8, 1892
43. Ibid.
44. Markus and Merritt, pp. 16–18
45. Karl Marx and Frederick Engels, *Letters to Americans: 1848–1895: A Selection*, New York, 1953, p. 253
46. London *Times*, May 2, 1893
47. Trachtenberg, p. 14
48. *Verhandlungen und Beschlüss des Internationalen Arbeiter-Kongresses zu Brussels*, 16–22, August 1891, Berlin pp. 30–31; Fricke, *Kleine Geschichte*, p. 46
49. *Protokoll des Internationalen Sozialistischen Arbeiter Kongresses in der Tonhalle Zürich vom 6, bis 12, August, 1893*, Zürich, 1894, pp. 30–37; Fricke, *Kleine Geschichte*, pp. 47–48
50. Philip S. Foner, *History of the Labor Movement in the United States* (New York, 1955)2: 235
51. Ibid.
52. Ibid., pp. 241–43; Donald L. McMurray, *Coxey's Army: A Study of the Industrial Army Movement of 1894*, Boston, 1929, pp. 110–16, 167
53. *The People*, May 6, 1894
54. Ibid.
55. Ibid.
56. London *Times*, May 2, 1894
57. Ibid.
58. Ibid.
59. Ibid.
60. Ibid.
61. London *Times*, May 2, 1895
62. Fricke, "The First Decade of May Day in the German Working Class," p. 9
63. Ibid.
64. T. Zagladina, "Las Primeras Acciones de los Obreros Rusos El Primera de Mayo," in *El Primero 1⁰ de Mayo en el Mundo*, vol. 2, pp. 242–45
65. "Lenin Manifesto for May 1, 1896," *Daily Worker*, April 18, 1929
66. Trachtenberg, p. 16
67. *New York Times*, April 30, 1944
68. Fricke, "The First Decade of May Day in the German Working Class," pp. 11–14
69. London *Times*, May 2, 1897, 1904, 1905
70. *The People*, May 2, 1893
71. Quoted in Trachtenberg, p. 19
72. Dieter Fricke, editor, *Dokumente Zum Deutschen Geschichte 1897/98–1904*, Berlin, 1976, p. 27

73. Adolf Braun, *Zum Arbstudententag, Historisches und Agitforisches uber Arbeiterschutz und Achstudentag*, Berlin, 1901, p. 37; Trachtenberg, p. 19
74. Adelman, p. 29
75. London *Times*, May 2, 1905
76. *New York Times*, May 2, 1905
77. Ibid., May 2, 1909
78. Ibid., May 2,3, 1909
79. London *Times*, May 2, 1910
80. Ibid., April 29-May 2, 1910
81. *New York Times*, May 2, 1910
82. London *Times*, May 2, 1911
83. Trachtenberg, p. 19
84. "The Bloody May Days of Tsarist Russia," *Daily Worker*, May 6, 1929
85. Jama Lazeron, " 'The Workingman's Hour': The 1886 Uprising in Boston," *Labor History* 21 (Spring, 1980): 216–17; Boston *Globe*, May 2, Sept. 6, 1886; Boston *Herald*, May 2, Sept. 7, 1886
86. *New York Times*, May 2, 1901
87. New York *Tribune*, September 12, 1894
88. American Federationist 3 (May, 1897): 52
89. *Proceedings*, AFL Convention, 1898, p. 21
90. Mary Cahill, *Shorter Hours*, New York, 1932, p. 186
91. Philip S. Foner, *History of the Labor Movement in the United States* 3 (New York, 1964): 120–34
92. *The Worker*, April 20, 1906; April 27, 1907
93. Joseph Schlossberg, "Meaning of the First of May," *Industrial Union Bulletin*, April 27, 1907
94. *Industrial Union Bulletin*, May 18, 1908; *Industrial Worker*, April 27, 1911
95. *Industrial Worker*, November 9, 1910
96. Ibid., Oct. 12, 1911; Foner, History of the Labor Movement in the U.S. 4 (New York, 1965):138–140
97. Foner, 4:436–38
98. *Industrial Union Bulletin*, April 27, 1907
99. *Industrial Worker*, May 4, 1911
100. New York *Call*, May 1, 1909
101. Ibid., May 2, 1909
102. *New York Times*, May 2, 1910
103. Ibid., May 2, 1911
104. Ibid., May 2, 1913
105. Ibid., May 2, 1914
106. El Primer 1⁰ de Mayo en el Mundo (Mexico City, 1981) 1:97–156; 173–204; 2:159–71

Chapter 5

1. *American Socialist*, August 15, 1914
2. *New York Times*, May 2, 1911
3. Merele Farsod, *International Socialism and the World War*, Cambridge, Mass., 1935
4. *New York Times*, May 2, 1915
5. Philip S. Foner, *Karl Liebknecht and the United States*, Chicago, 1978, pp. 14–16
6. Fricke, *Kleine Geschichte*, pp. 157–58
7. Foner, *Karl Liebknecht*, pp. 22–24
8. Karl Liebknecht, *The Future Belongs to the People*, New York, 1918, p. 85

9. Richard M. Watt, *The Kings Depart, The Tragedy of Germany: Versailles & the German Revolution*, New York, 1968, pp. 129–30
10. Fricke, *Kleine Geschichte*, p. 158
11. *New York Times*, May 2, 1917; London *Times*, May 2, 1917
12. *New York Times*, May 2, 1917
13. London *Times*, May 2, 1917; Fricke, *Kleine Geschichte*, pp. 166–67
14. Fricke, *Kleine Geschichte*, p. 172
15. London *Times*, May 6, 1918
16. *New York Times*, May 2, 1916
17. Ibid.
18. *Cleveland Plain Dealer*, May 2, 1917
19. *New York Times*, May 2, 1917
20. *New York Times*, May 4, 1918
21. *Chicago Tribune*, May 2, 1918
22. Robert K. Murray, *Red Scare: A Study in National Hysteria, 1919–1920*, Minneapolis, 1955, pp. 72–73
23. Boston *Evening Transcript*, May 2, June 15, 1919; Murray, p. 74
24. *New York Times*, May 2, 1919
25. "May Day Rioting," *Nation* CVIII (May 10, 1919); New York *Call*, May 2, 1919; *New York Times*, May 2, 1919; Murray, p. 75
26. *Cleveland Plain Dealer*, May 2, 1919
27. Ibid.
28. *Canada's Party of Socialism, History of the Communist Party of Canada, 1921–1976*, Progress Publishers, Toronto, 1982, pp. 12–13
29. V.I. Lenin, *Drei Reden auf dem Rote Platz, 1, Mai, 1919, Werke*, vol. 29, p. 317; Fricke, *Kleine Geschichte*, p. 179
30. *New York Times*, May 2, 1919; Herbert Steiner, "First May Day in Austria," p. 8. Copy of unpublished paper in possession of present writer.
31. London *Times*, May 2, 1919
32. *New York Times*, May 3, 1919
33. Reprinted in ibid.
34. *New York Times*, May 2, 1919
35. London *Times*, May 2, 1919
36. Foner, *Karl Liebknecht*, pp. 55–57; Fricke, *Kleine Geschichte*, p. 182
37. London *Times*, May 2, 1919
38. Ibid.
39. Ibid.
40. *New York Times*, May 2, 1919
41. Robert W. Dunn, *The Palmer Raids*, New York, 1952
42. *New York Times*, May 1, 2, 1920
43. London *Times*, May 2, 1920
44. Ibid.
45. Ibid.
46. New York Times, May 2, 1920
47. London *Times*, May 2, 1920
48. Ibid.
49. *New York Times*, May 1, 2, 1920; London *Times*, May 2, 1920
50. Fricke, *Kleine Geschichte*, p. 188
51. *New York Times*, May 2, 1920
52. Ruyji Komatsu and Ichiro Saga, "First May Day in Japan," pp. 4–11
53. *New York Times*, April 25, 1921, April 26, 1922
54. *New York Times*, April 29, 1921
55. Ibid., April 29, 30, May 1, 1921
56. *New York Times*, May 2–4, 1921; *Chicago Tribune*, May 2, 1921
57. *New York Times*, May 2, 1921; London *Times*, May 2, 1921
58. *New York Times*, May 2, 1925

59. Ibid.; *Daily Worker*, May 2, 1925
60. *New York Times*, April 30, 1925
61. Ibid., May 1, 1925
62. London *Times*, May 2, 1925
63. Ibid., April 25, 1926
64. London *Times*, May 2, 1926
65. Ibid.
66. Ibid., May 2, 3, 1926
67. *New York Times*, July 12, 1926
68. Ibid., May 2, 1926
69. Ibid.
70. Ibid.
71. Ibid., May 2, 1923
72. Ibid., May 2, 1926
73. Ibid.
74. Ibid., April 24, 1927
75. Ibid., May 2, 1927; *Daily Worker*, May 2, 1927
76. *Boston Globe*, May 2, 1927; *New York Times*, May 2, 1927
77. *New York Times*, May 1, 2, 3, 1927
78. *New York Times*, May 2, 1927
79. London *Times*, May 2, 1927; *New York Times*, May 2, 1927
80. London *Times*, May 2, 1927
81. Ibid.
82. *New York Times*, May 4, 1927
83. Ibid., May 8, 1927
84. Dilip Bose, *May Day and the Indian Working Class*, New Delhi, 1979, pp. 25–29
85. *New York Times*, May 2, 1928
86. London *Times*, May 2, 1928
87. *New York Times*, May 2, 1928
88. Ibid., May 1, 1928
89. Ibid.
90. Ibid., May 1, 1929
91. Ibid., May 2, 1929
92. London *Times*, May 2, 1929
93. *New York Times*, May 1, 2, 1929
94. London *Times*, May 2, 1929; *New York Times*, May 2, 1929
95. *New York Times*, May 2, 1929; Fricke, *Kleine Geschichte*, p. 208; London *Times*, May 2, 1929
96. *Daily Worker*, May 13, 1929
97. *Diario de la Marina*, May 2–5, 1929; Harrison George, "Cuba's Proletariat Battles on May Day," *Daily Worker*, May 18, 1929

Chapter 6

1. *New York Times*, May 2, 1926, May 3 1928
2. Philip S. Foner, *Organized Labor and the Black Worker, 1619–1981*, New York, 1981, p. 188
3. Fricke, *Kleine Geschichte*, p. 209
4. *Daily Worker*, March 8, 1930, April 12, 1931
5. Frances Fox Piven and Richard A. Cloward, *Regulating the Poor*, New York, 197, p. 60; Arthur M. Schlesinger, Jr., *The Crisis of the Old Order*, Boston, 1957, pp. 166, 207, 219
6. Schlesinger, Jr., p. 124
7. *Daily Worker*, October 15, 1929, March 7–8, 1930; *New York Times*, March 7,

1930; Daniel J. Leab, " 'United We Eat': The Creation and Organization of the Unemployed Councils in 1930," *Labor History* 8 (Fall, 1976): 299–300; Albert Prago, "The Organization of the Unemployed and the Role of the Radicals, 1929–1935," Ph.D. diss., American University, 1976, pp. 32–35

8. Prago, pp. 61–63; *New York Times*, March 7, 1930; *Daily Worker*, March 7–8, 1930
9. New York *World*, March 7, 1930; *Daily Worker*, March 7, July 31, 1930
10. *Labor Defender*, May, 1930, p. 91
11. *New York Times*, May 2, 1930
12. Ibid.
13. London *Times*, May 2, 1930
14. *New York Times*, May 2, 1930; *Chicago Tribune*, May 2, 1930; Philadelphia *North American*, May 2, 1930
15. *Canada's Party of Socialism*, p. 92
16. *Daily Worker* (London), May 1, 1930; London *Times*, May 2, 1930
17. London *Times*, May 2, 1930
18. *New York Times*, May 2, 1930
19. Ibid.
20. Ibid.
21. Ibid.
22. Ibid.
23. London *Times*, May 2, 1931
24. *New York Times*, May 2, 1931
25. London *Times*, May 2, 1931
26. *New York Times*, May 2, 1931
27. *Daily Worker*, May 2, 1932; *New York Times*, May 2, 1932
28. *New York Times*, April 25, May 1, 1933
29. Ibid., May 2, 1933
30. London *Times*, May 2, 1933
31. Fricke, *Kleine Geschichte*, pp. 224–26; Manfred Weissbecker, *Gegen Faschismus und Kriegsgefahr. Ein Beitrag zur Geschichte der KPD in Thüringen, 1933–1935*, Erfurt, 1967, pp. 50–52
32. *New York Times*, May 3, 1933
33. Ibid., April 30, May 1, 2, 1933; *Daily Worker*, May 1, 2, 1933
34. London *Times*, May 2, 1933
35. *New York Times*, May 1, 1934; London *Times*, May 2, 1934
36. Quoted in Herbert Steiner, "The First May Day in Austria," unpublished paper in possession of present writer, pp. 8–9
37. Ibid.
38. Ibid., p. 9
39. *New York Times*, May 2, 1934; *Daily Worker*, May 2, 1934
40. London *Times*, May 2, 1934
41. *New York Times*, May 2, 1935; *Daily Worker*, May 2, 1935
42. *Canada's Party of Socialism*, pp. 92–95
43. *Daily Worker*, May 1, 1936; *New York Times*, May 1, 1936.
44. *New York Times*, May 2, 1936; *Daily Worker*, May 1, 2, 1936; Michael H. Frisch and Daniel J. Walkowitz, ed., *Working-Class America: Essays in Labor, Community, and American Society*, Urbana, Ill., 1983, pp. 264–266
45. *Daily Worker*, May 2, 1936
46. *New York Times*, May 2, 1936
47. *Daily Worker*, May 2, 1936; *New York Times*, May 2, 1936
48. Ryuji Komatsu and Ichiro Saga, "First May Day in Japan," p. 12
49. *New York Times*, May 2, 1936
50. London *Times*, May 2, 1936
51. Sidney Fine, *Sit-Down: The General Motors Strike of 1936–1937*, Ann Arbor, Michigan, 1969

52. *New York Times*, April 27, 1937
53. Ibid., May 2, 1937; London *Times*, May 2, 1937
54. *New York Times*, May 2, 1937; *Chicago Tribune*, May 2, 1937
55. London *Times*, May 3, 1937
56. *New York Times*, May 6, 1937
57. Ibid., May 1, 1938
58. Ibid., May 2, 1938
59. Ibid.
60. Ibid.; *Daily Worker*, May 2, 1938
61. London *Times*, May 2, 1938
62. Ibid.
63. *New York Times*, May 2, 1938
64. Ibid; London *Times*, May 2, 1938
65. *New York Times*, May 2, 1938
66. Reprinted in Fricke, *Kleine Geschichte*, p. 233
67. Geoffrey Barraclough, *The Origins of Modern Germany*, New York, 1979, p. 453
68. London *Times*, May 2, 1940
69. Ibid., May 2, 1942
70. *New York Times*, May 1, 2, 1942
71. Ibid., May 6, 1942
72. Ibid., April 26, May 3, 1942; Fricke, *Kleine Geschichte*, p. 240
73. *New York Times*, May 5, 1943
74. Ibid., May 1, 1943
75. London *Times*, May 3, 1943
76. *New York Times*, April 29, May 3, 1943; *Daily Worker*, May 2, 3, 1943
77. Wilhelm Pieck, "Zum Mai," in *Gessamelte Reden und Schriften*, Berlin, 1979, vol. 6, p. 255
78. Fricke, *Kleine Geschichte*, pp. 245–46
79. *New York Times*, April 30, 1944
80. Ibid., May 2, 1944
81. Ibid., April 28, 1944
82. Ibid., May 3, 1944
83. Quoted in Steiner, p. 10
84. *New York Times*, May 2, 1945

Chapter 7

1. London *Times*, May 2, 1946
2. Fricke, *Kleine Geschichte*, p. 255
3. Ibid., p. 256
4. London *Times*, May 1, 2, 1946
5. *Amsterdam News*, May 4, 1946; *The Hawspipe*, Newsletter of the Marine Workers Historical Association, May, 1984, pp. 1, 10–11
6. Ibid.; *Daily Worker*, May 2, 1946
7. *New York Times*, May 2, 1946; *Daily Worker*, May 2, 1946
8. *New York Times*, May 2, 1946
9. Ibid.
10. Ibid.; Ryuyi Tomatsu and Ichiro Saga, "First May Day in Japan," p. 11
11. *New York Times*, May 2, 1946
12. Dilip Bose, *May Day and the Indian Working Class*, New Delhi, 1979, pp. 55–56
13. *New York Times*, May 2, 1946
14. Ibid., December 5, 1947
15. Ibid., May 2, 1920
16. Ibid., April 27, 1921; May 1, 1923

17. Trachtenberg, pp. 21–22
18. Richard O. Boyer and Herbert M. Morais, *Labor's Untold Story*, pp. 324–27; *New York Herald Tribune*, January 29, March 24, 1950; New York *Compass*, February 1, 1950
19. *New York Times*, April 20, 1948
20. Ibid., May 2, 1949
21. Ibid., May 1,2, 1948
22. Ibid., April 30, 1955
23. Ibid., April 30, May 1, 1948
24. Ibid., May 1, 1949, May 1, 2, 1950, May 2, 1951
25. Ibid., May 2, 1948
26. *New York Times*, April 30, May 1, 1950
27. *Daily Worker*, April 29, 1951; *New York Times*, May 2, 1951
28. *Daily Worker*, May 2, 1951; *New York Times*, May 2, 1951
29. London *Times*, May 2, 1949
30. *New York Times*, April 26, 29, 1953
31. Boyer and Morais, pp. 350–56; David Caute, *The Great Fear*, London, 1978, pp. 112–48
32. Ibid., April 29, 1953
33. Ibid., April 30, 1953
34. Ibid.
35. Ibid., May 4, 1953
36. *Daily Worker*, May 2, 1953; *New York Times*, May 2, 1953
37. *New York Times*, April 4, 16, 1954
38. *Daily Worker*, May 3, 1954
39. *New York Times*, April 30, 1955; *Daily Worker*, May 2, 1955
40. *New York Times*, April 13, 1956
41. Ibid., May 1,2, 1956; *Daily Worker*, May 2, 1956
42. *New York Times*, May 2, 1957; *Daily Worker*, May 3, 1957
43. *Daily Worker*, May 3, 1957
44. Ibid., April 30, May 1, 1958; *New York Times*, May 1, 1958
45. *New York Times*, April 30, May 3, 1959
46. Ibid., May 3, 1959
47. London *Times*, May 2, 1955
48. Ibid., May 2, 1958
49. Ibid.
50. Ibid., May 2, 1956
51. *New York Times*, May 2, 1958
52. Ibid., April 30, 1950
53. Ibid., May 2, 1950; Ken Luckhardt and Brenda Wall, *Organize or Starve! The History of the South Africa Congress of Trade Unions*, New York, 1980, pp. 333–34
54. Ibid., May 2, 1950; April 30, 1951
55. Ibid., May 2, 1951
56. Ibid., April 6, 1954
57. Ibid., April 21, 1955
58. Ibid., December 26, 1959
59. London *Times*, May 2, 1953
60. *New York Times*, May 2, 1954; April 28, 1955
61. London *Times*, May 2, 1952; *New York Times*, May 2, 1952
62. *New York Times*, October 16, 1955
63. Ibid., May 1, 1954
64. Ibid., May 2, 1956
65. Ibid., April 22, 1956
66. London *Times*, May 2, 1953
67. *New York Times*, May 2, 1954, May 2, 1956

68. Ibid., April 25, 1958
69. Ibid., May 2, 1959
70. London *Times*, May 2, 1959
71. *New York Times*, May 2, 1952
72. Ibid.
73. London *Times*, May 3, 1954
74. *New York Times*, April 12, May 2, 1955
75. Ibid., May 2, 1959
76. London *Times*, May 3, 1954; *New York Times*, April 3, 1956
77. E. R. Braverman, "The Story of May Day in South Africa," *New Age*, April 26, 1956, p. 5

Chapter 8

1. *New York Times*, April 23 1961; May 2 1962
2. Ibid., May 2, 1963
3. Ibid., May 2, 1962
4. *New York Times*, May 1, 1962
5. Ibid., May 2, 1964
6. Ibid., May 2, 1965
7. Ibid.
8. London *Times*, May 3, 1965
9. *New York Times*, May 2, 1966
10. *Canada's Party of Socialism*, pp. 266–7.
11. *New York Times*, May 2, 1967
12. Ibid., May 2, 1968
13. London *Times*, May 2, 1968
14. London *Times*, May 2, 1968; *New York Times*, May 5, 1969
15. *New York Times*, May 2, 1975; London *Times*, May 2, 1975
16. *New York Times*, April 30 May 2,3, 1961
17. Ibid., May 2, 1965
18. Ibid., May 2, 1972
19. Paul E. Sigmund, *The Overthrow of Allende and the Politics Of Chile*, 1964–1976, Pittsburgh, 1977, pp. 231–47
20. London *Times*, May 2, 1978; *New York Times*, May 2, 1978
21. *New York Times*, May 2, 1979
22. London *Times*, May 2, 1974
23. *New York Times*, May 2, 1977
24. London *Times*, May 2, 1977
25. *New York Times*, May 2, 1976
26. Ibid., May 2, 1977
27. London *Daily Telegraph*, May 2, 1979; *New York Times*, May 2, 1979
28. London *Daily Telegraph*, May 2, 1979; *New York Times*, May 2, 1979
29. Fricke, *Kleine Geschichte*, p. 271
30. London *Times*, May 2, 1971; *New York Times*, May 2, 1971
31. *New York Times*, May 2, 1973
32. *Daily World*, April 27, 1978
33. *Daily World*, April 30, May 1, 1977
34. Statement issued by Committee for a United Labor and People's May Day, *Daily World*, April 30, May 1, 1978
35. *Daily World*, April 30, May 2, 1978; *New York Times*, April 30, 1978
36. London *Times*, May 2, 1981
37. Ibid; *New York Times*, May 2, 1981
38. Call for May Day Conference; copy of leaflet in possession of present writer; *New York Times*, May 2, 1982

39. *New York Times*, May 2, 1983; London *Times*, May 2, 1983
40. *New York Times*, May 2, 1984; London *Times*, May 2, 1984
41. *New York Times*, July 2,5,10, 1985
42. *Labor Today*, May, 1985
43. *Daily World*, May 18, 1985
44. Copy of leaflet in possession of present writer
45. *Daily World*, May 18, 1985
46. *Labor Today*, May, 1985
47. Ibid.
48. Ibid.
49. *The Worker*, May 29, 1951
50. Quoted in *In These Times*, August 6–12, 1977

Index